Amazing Love!
How Can It Be

Amazing Love! How Can It Be

Studies on Hymns by Charles Wesley

edited by
CHRIS FENNER
BRIAN G. NAJAPFOUR
foreword by David W. Music

RESOURCE *Publications* • Eugene, Oregon

AMAZING LOVE! HOW CAN IT BE
Studies on Hymns by Charles Wesley

Copyright © 2020 Chris Fenner and Brian G. Najapfour. All rights reserved. Except for brief quotations in critical publications or reviews, no part of this book may be reproduced in any manner without prior written permission from the publisher. Write: Permissions, Wipf and Stock Publishers, 199 W. 8th Ave., Suite 3, Eugene, OR 97401.

Resource Publications
An Imprint of Wipf and Stock Publishers
199 W. 8th Ave., Suite 3
Eugene, OR 97401

www.wipfandstock.com

PAPERBACK ISBN: 978-1-7252-6475-5
HARDCOVER ISBN: 978-1-7252-6476-2
EBOOK ISBN: 978-1-7252-6477-9

Library of Congress Classification:
BV312.F4 or BX8495.W4.F4

Manufactured in the U.S.A.   04/27/20

Dedicated to
Esther R. Crookshank,
whose love for hymnology
inspired our own.

Contents

Foreword by David W. Music   ix

Contributors   xi

CONVERSION

1 | Where shall my wondering soul begin?   3
    Brian G. Najapfour

2 | And can it be that I should gain   11
    Steve Weaver

3 | O for a thousand tongues to sing   18
    Jonathan A. Powers

STRUGGLE & RESPITE

4 | Jesu, lover of my soul   29
    Patrick A. Eby & Christopher P. McFadden

5 | Come, O thou traveller unknown (Wrestling Jacob)   36
    C. Michael Hawn

INCARNATION & RESURRECTION

6 | Come, Thou long-expected Jesus   47
    Josh Dear

7 | Hark! the herald angels sing   59
    Chris Fenner

8 | Christ the Lord is ris'n today   64
    Joe Harrod

ORDINANCES & SANCTIFICATION

9 | The Means of Grace   73
    Chris Fenner

10| O the depth of love divine   79
    Paul W. Chilcote

11| Love divine, all loves excelling   86
    Roger D. Duke & Chris Fenner

A PRAYER OF EVANGELISM

12| Sun of unclouded righteousness   97
    Michael A.G. Haykin

HYMN TUNES & HYMNALS

13| Operatic influences on the hymn tunes used by John and Charles Wesley   111
    Margaret Garrett

14| A Baptist preacher and a Methodist hymnal   130
    Jim Scott Orrick

Appendix: A Collection of Tunes as They Were Used by the Wesleys   139

Bibliography   177

Subject Index   183

Collections and Hymns Index   187

Scripture Index   191

Foreword

DAVID W. MUSIC

Charles Wesley is universally recognized as one of the greatest writers of hymns in the English language. Widely anthologized in hymnals, sung in churches, and meditated upon in private devotions, Wesley's hymns have spoken to Christians in many different generations, countries, denominations, and life situations.

The hymns of Wesley still speak profoundly today. It is difficult to imagine an Advent or Christmas season without "Hark, the herald angels sing" or a Resurrection Sunday without "Christ the Lord is risen today." How could we do without "And can it be," "Jesu, lover of my soul," "Love divine, all loves excelling," or "O for a thousand tongues to sing"? And these are just the proverbial tip of the iceberg!

And yet, for all the singing of Charles Wesley's hymns, only in recent years has the sort of serious attention paid to his brother John been accorded to Charles and his work. As late as 1948, Frank Baker wrote, "Charles Wesley is not as well known, even amongst Methodists, as he deserves to be.... The main reason for the comparative neglect of Charles Wesley is, of course, John Wesley. John has completely overshadowed his younger brother."[1]

Thanks to the pioneering efforts of Baker and others, that situation has changed, and Charles Wesley and his hymns have begun to receive the sort of attention they deserve. There have been several important biographical studies, as well as excellent discussions of the hymns in a larger context, including Madeleine Forell Marshall and Janet Todd's *English Congregational Hymns in the Eighteenth Century* (1982), Donald Davie's *The Eighteenth-Century Hymn in England* (1993), and J.R. Watson's magisterial *The English Hymn: A Critical and Historical Study* (1997). Fine works have

---

1. Frank Baker, *Charles Wesley as Revealed by His Letters* (London: Epworth Press, 1948) 1.

been published dealing with his hymns on specific topics or those found in special collections, such as Daniel B. Stevick's *The Altar's Fire: Charles Wesley's Hymns on the Lord's Supper, 1745* (2004). Likewise, the facsimile and critical editions of Wesleyan hymn collections have added significantly to our understanding of the poet and his work, including projects such as S.T. Kimbrough and Oliver A. Beckerlegge's *The Unpublished Poetry of Charles Wesley* (1988–1992). Yet—and this is the mark of a great artist—there is always room for further exploration of Wesley and his impact on the community of faith.

Scholarship on Charles Wesley particularly stands to benefit from in-depth studies of individual hymns. In his *Hermeneutics of Hymnody: A Comprehensive and Integrated Approach to Understanding Hymns* (2015), Scotty Gray pointed out several dimensions of hymnody ripe for study and analysis: its relationship to the Bible, theology, liturgy, poetry, and music; its historical, biographical, and sociocultural aspects; and its practice. The study of each element in isolation is important, but it is only when these different facets are "integrated" (Gray's word) that a hymn can be fully understood.

The present collection of essays on twelve of Wesley's hymns (and other related topics) does this. Each essay examines a specific text by Wesley in its multiple dimensions, demonstrating both the profound nature of the hymn and its continued relevance for Christians today. The discussions are organized by theological/liturgical topics, and each treats us to the hymn in its complete original form (noting significant variants from later publications), provides a theological interpretation of the text, and relates it to the life and faith of the believer. Nor are the musical, educational, and devotional dimensions of the hymns neglected.

In the pages of this book, the reader will find both information and inspiration. Scholars of hymnody and of Charles Wesley will appreciate the depth of the inquiry in the chapters. Just as importantly, laypersons and hymn lovers (as well as scholars) will find much spiritual benefit from the study of hymns they know and love, as well as texts with which they may be less familiar. This exploration of these profound hymns will surely lead to a deeper understanding of the "amazing love" responsible for changing the course of Charles Wesley's life, who in turn changed the course of Christian worship.

DAVID W. MUSIC
Professor of Church Music
Baylor University

Contributors

PAUL W. CHILCOTE is a retired professor of historical theology and Wesleyan studies who has served in a number of seminaries in faculty and administrative roles. He taught at St. Paul's Theological College (Kenya) and helped launch United Methodist-related Africa University (Zimbabwe). He served a president of The Charles Wesley Society for eight years. Author of nearly thirty books, he received the Saddlebag Award for his book *A Faith That Sings: Biblical Themes in the Lyrical Theology of Charles Wesley* (Wipf & Stock, 2016).

ROGER D. DUKE retired early from Baptist College of Health Sciences after eighteen years of classroom teaching ministry. He received his doctorate from The University of the South at Sewanee and subsequently taught at various colleges and graduate schools. Duke has authored or contributed to volumes on John Albert Broadus, John Bunyan, William Carey, Basil Manly Jr., and Pope John Paul II.

PATRICK A. EBY is an Associate Professor of Church History and Christian Ministry at Wesley Seminary in Marion, Indiana, and is an ordained minister in the Wesleyan Church. He is President of the Charles Wesley Society and serves in leadership positions in the Wesleyan Theological Society and the Wesleyan Historical Society. He is the author of *The Heart of Charles Wesley's Theology* and coauthor of the book *How God Makes the World a Better Place: A Wesleyan Primer on Faith, Work, and Economic Transformation*.

JOSH DEAR is a native of Jackson, Mississippi, where he formerly taught Bible classes at Belhaven University and managed the bookstore at Reformed Theological Seminary. He earned a BA in Biblical Studies from Belhaven University and an MDiv from Beeson Divinity School, and he has served as an associate pastor for several Baptist churches. Josh co-authored the book *Crossing the Tracks* (Kregel, 2012), as well as a chapter for the book *The Beauty and Glory of Christian*

Living (Reformation Heritage Books, 2016), and he served as an editor for Randy Alcorn's book *Happiness* (Tyndale, 2015). He lives in West Michigan with his wife and three children, where he serves as Shelter Supervisor for Muskegon Rescue Mission.

CHRIS FENNER is Digital Archivist at The Southern Baptist Theological Seminary and is Assoc. Minister of Music at Green Street Baptist Church, Louisville, Kentucky. He has degrees in Music Education, Worship Studies, and Library Science. Chris has contributed scholarly articles to *The Hymn: A Journal of Congregational Song*, has produced new editions of the *Psalms, Hymns, and Spiritual Songs of Isaac Watts* and *Our Own Hymn-Book* by Charles Spurgeon, and is managing editor of HymnologyArchive.com.

MARGARET GARRETT is Associate Professor of Voice at Ouachita Baptist University, where she teaches Studio Voice and Vocal Literature. She has performed as a recitalist, an oratorio soloist, an orchestral soloist, and in opera and musical theatre across the United States and in Germany. Garrett holds a Doctor of Musical Arts degree in Voice Performance from The Southern Baptist Theological Seminary, a Master of Music degree in Voice Performance from Indiana University-Bloomington, a Bachelor of Music degree in Voice Performance from the University of North Carolina School of the Arts, and a high school diploma with concentrations in voice and harp from the Baltimore School for the Arts.

JOSEPH C. HARROD is Assistant Professor of Biblical Spirituality and Associate Vice President for Institutional Effectiveness at The Southern Baptist Theological Seminary in Louisville, Kentucky. A Senior Fellow of the Andrew Fuller Center for Baptist Studies, he is an editor for the Andrew Fuller Works project. His most recent publication is *Theology and Spirituality in the Works of Samuel Davies* (Vandenhoeck & Ruprecht, 2019).

C. MICHAEL HAWN is University Distinguished Professor Emeritus of Church Music and Director of the Doctor of Pastoral Music degree program, Perkins School of Theology, Southern Methodist University. A Fellow of the Hymn Society in the United States and Canada, he has been the primary writer and editor of the weekly *History of Hymns* column for the United Methodist Discipleship Ministries website since 2004 and is the USA editor for the *Canterbury Dictionary of Hymnology* since 2017. His most recent book is *New Songs of Celebration Render: Congregational Song in the Twenty-first Century* (GIA, 2013).

MICHAEL A. G. HAYKIN is Chair and Professor of Church History at The Southern Baptist Theological Seminary and Director of the Andrew Fuller Center for Baptist Studies. Haykin has a BA in Philosophy from the University of Toronto (1974), a Master of Religion from Wycliffe College, the University of Toronto (1977), and a ThD in Church History from Wycliffe College and the University of Toronto (1982). Haykin and his wife, Alison, have two grown children: Victoria and Nigel.

CHRISTOPHER P. MCFADDEN is pastor of Lakin Wesleyan Church and a doctoral student at Wesley Seminary in Marion, Indiana, and is an ordained minister in the Wesleyan Church. He is currently working toward a Doctor of Ministry in Spiritual Formation. Chris earned a Bachelor of Science in Pastoral Ministry at Oklahoma Wesleyan University in 2006. He completed his Master of Divinity degree at Wesley Seminary in 2018. He most recently presented a paper entitled "Preaching the resurrection as a foretaste of heaven: Charles Wesley's hymns of the resurrection as eschatology" at the Wesleyan Theological Society in March 2019.

BRIAN G. NAJAPFOUR holds a ThM degree in Historical Theology from Puritan Reformed Theological Seminary, Grand Rapids, Michigan. He has been a minister of the gospel since 2001 and has served both in the Philippines and the U.S. He is the author of numerous books including *Amazing Grace*, the first part of the series called "Stories behind Favorite Hymns for Ages 3 to 6." He is currently pursuing a PhD in Biblical Spirituality at The Southern Baptist Theological Seminary, Louisville, Kentucky. His areas of research include hymnology. He and his wife Sarah have four children.

JIM SCOTT ORRICK is a professor at Boyce College and the lead pastor at Bullitt Lick Baptist Church. His PhD is in English Literature. He composed the music for and recorded *The Baptist Catechism Set to Music*. He has contributed chapters to books on literature, philosophy, history, and theology. He co-authored *Encountering God Through Expository Preaching*, and he is the author of *A Year With George Herbert* and *Mere Calvinism*.

JONATHAN A. POWERS is Assistant Professor of Worship at Asbury Theological Seminary. He graduated from Asbury University in 2003 with a BA in English, from Asbury Theological Seminary in 2009 with an MA in Christian Ministries (worship studies emphasis), and holds the Doctor of Worship Studies from The Robert E. Webber Institute for Worship Studies in Jacksonville, Florida. He is currently writing a PhD dissertation through The London School of Theology on the worship theology of Robert E. Webber. Dr. Powers has a passion for the intersection of liturgy and spiritual formation in the life of the church. He has authored and co-authored several articles and books, including *Echo: A Catechism for Discipleship in the Ancient Christian Tradition*, *The 12 Days of Christmas Sermons*, and *Watchnight: John Wesley's Covenant Renewal Service*.

STEVE WEAVER has been the pastor of Farmdale Baptist Church in Frankfort, Kentucky, since 2008. He also serves as a Fellow for The Andrew Fuller Center for Baptist Studies at The Southern Baptist Theological Seminary, where he is an adjunct professor of church history. He is a graduate of Liberty University (BS, 2002) and The Southern Baptist Theological Seminary (MDiv, 2005; PhD, 2013). Steve is the author of *Orthodox, Puritan, Baptist: Hercules Collins (1647–1702) and Particular Baptist Identity in Early Modern England* (Vandenhoeck & Ruprecht, 2015). Steve and his wife Gretta have been married for over twenty years and have been blessed with six children.

Conversion

1

Where shall my wondering soul begin?

BRIAN G. NAJAPFOUR

Born on December 18, 1707, in Epworth, Lincolnshire, England, Charles Wesley grew up in an Anglican family. In 1726, he entered Christ Church College at Oxford University, where he received his BA (1730) and MA (1733). At Oxford in 1729 he started the Holy Club, a religious organization promoting piety through systematic study of the Bible, prayer, fasting, Communion, and other religious acts. In 1735, Charles was ordained an Anglican priest, and that same year he and his brother John (1703–1791) journeyed to the newly founded colony of Georgia to help spread and develop Anglicanism there, especially among the Native Americans. When their mission was unsuccessful, they were compelled to return to England—first Charles in late 1736, followed by John in early 1738. Despite this failure, however, this mission trip became memorable to the brothers. During this period they met the Moravians, who had a profound impact on their pursuit of personal conversion and their passion for hymns.

On May 21, 1738, despite being raised and trained in the Church and devoted to ritual holiness, Charles Wesley experienced evangelical conversion, which he expressed this way: "I now found myself at peace with God, and rejoiced in hope of loving Christ."[1] Two days later, he wrote what he called "an hymn upon my conversion."[2] Although Wesley did not name the hymn in his journal, scholars generally believe it was "Where shall my

---

1. Kimbrough and Newport, *Manuscript Journal*, 1:108 (21 May 1738).
2. Kimbrough and Newport, *Manuscript Journal*, 1:109 (23 May 1738).

wondering soul begin?" This hymn, originally titled "Christ the Friend of Sinners," was first published the following year in *Hymns and Sacred Poems* (1739), in eight stanzas of six lines. It was revised in 1743, 1761, and 1780.[3]

STANZA 1

> Where shall my wond'ring[4] soul begin?
>   How shall I all to heav'n aspire?
> A slave redeemed from death and sin,
>   A brand plucked from eternal fire;
> How shall I equal triumphs raise,
> Or[5] sing my great Deliverer's praise!

Amazed by his life-changing experience of redeeming grace, Charles Wesley opened his hymn by asking rhetorically, "Where shall my wondering soul begin? How shall I all to heaven aspire?" The hymnist was astonished the most glorious God would redeem a "slave" like him. Wesley indicated his humility by considering himself a slave, the lowest of the low in society. Some of his readers might have found this language jarring; especially the clergymen who thought highly of themselves, or the members of lower classes who saw their religious leaders as elevated or superior. But what really struck Wesley with wonder was God's redemption of an insignificant person like him from sin and its wages, which is death in eternal fire. His choice of the word "redeemed" should not surprise us, for two reasons: first, it fits well with Wesley's self-portrait as a slave. A slave who has been purchased is redeemed, not just saved. Second, the day before Wesley wrote his hymn, he had been meditating on Isaiah 43:1–3.[6] The first of these verses reads, "But now thus saith the LORD that created thee, O Jacob, and he that formed thee, O Israel, Fear not: for I have redeemed thee, I have called thee by thy name; thou art mine" (KJV). Wesley's meditation on this passage led him to this conclusion: he wanted his readers and singers to know he was but a worthless slave redeemed by God's wonderful grace.

---

3. The hymn was revised in the 4th ed. of *Hymns and Sacred Poems* [HSP] (1743), repeated in *Hymns and Spiritual Songs* [HSS] (1753), reduced to the first four stanzas in *Hymns for Those to Whom Christ is All in All* [HTWCAA] (1761), then restored to seven stanzas in *A Collection of Hymns for the Use of the People Called Methodists* (1780), with minor corrections in 2nd ed. (1781); the sixth stanza was omitted in 1780 but is included here for reference and analysis. See Maddox, *Charles Wesley's Published Verse*.

4. wandering : *Collection*, 1st ed. (1780), corrected in 2nd ed. (1781).

5. And : HSP (1739, 1743); HSS (1753); HTWCAA (1761).

6. Kimbrough and Newport, *Manuscript Journal*, 1:108 (22 May 1738).

To further emphasize his worthlessness before God, Wesley compared himself to a "brand plucked from eternal fire," phrasing borrowed from Zechariah 3:2. His use of biblical words and phrases in this and other hymns is one of the earmarks of his hymnody—so much so, J. Ernest Rattenbury once remarked, "a skillful man, if the Bible were lost, might extract it from Wesley's hymns. They contain the Bible in solution."[7] This comment might be an exaggeration, but it demonstrates how Wesley's hymns are saturated with scriptural language. The fiery phrase was probably also an allusion to a significant moment in John Wesley's life, in which he was rescued from a fire in Epworth in 1709. Later in life, John commissioned a visual representation of the event, underscored by the words, "Is not this a brand plucked from the burning?"[8]

Having experienced this undeserved redemption, and pondering ways to express his heartfelt gratitude to the Lord, Charles could only exclaim, "How shall I . . . sing my great Deliverer's praise!" By implication, the celebrated hymnist was recognizing how the world's best hymns fall short of fully expressing gratitude for God's great work of salvation.

STANZA 2

> O how shall I thy[9] goodness tell!
>   Father, which thou to me hast showed,
> That I, a child of wrath and hell,
>   I should be called a child of God![10]
> Should know, should feel my sins forgiv'n,
> Blest with this antepast of heav'n!

Still thrilled by God's goodness, Wesley exclaimed prayerfully: "O how shall I the goodness tell! Father, which Thou to me hast showed." This goodness was expounded in the third and fourth lines: he who was once "a child of wrath and hell" is now by grace "a child of God." With the use of the personal pronouns "I," "my," and "me" throughout the stanza, Wesley was unveiling the experiential nature of adoption; it is a doctrine Christians experience personally.

For Methodist spirituality, the words "feel" and "know" in the fifth line are important. The former stresses how we can experience (feel) the Holy Spirit's regenerating work in us. The latter gives us confidence in knowing,

---

7. Rattenbury, *Conversions of the Wesleys*, 84.
8. Jacobs, *Epworth Herald*, 15.
9. the : *HSP* (1739, 1743); *HSS* (1753); *HTWCAA* (1761).
10. Should now be called a child of God! : *HTWCAA* (1761).

by this work, we are forgiven and we are God's children. This idea is rooted in Scriptures such as 1 John 3:1, "Behold, what manner of love the Father hath bestowed upon us, that we should be called the sons of God." Wesley ended his stanza on an eschatological tone. Our present experience of the doctrine of adoption is just an "antepast," or foretaste, of what we will fully enjoy in heaven someday.

STANZA 3

> And shall I slight my father's love?
>   Or basely fear his gifts to own?
> Unmindful of his favours prove?
>   Shall I, the hallowed cross to shun,
> Refuse his righteousness t'impart
> By hiding it within my heart?

Wesley filled his third stanza with rhetorical questions, expecting "no" for an answer. The first line teaches us our proper response to God for His love: praise. Anything short of this would slight his love. According to Wesley's journal, as he was composing this hymn, Satan kept discouraging him. The devil knew Wesley was going to write about the good things God had done for him in salvation. Opposing his desire to share his conversion story through the song, Satan made him think his composition would exalt his own sinful pride, not God's praise. Wesley wrote:

> At nine I began an hymn upon my conversion, but was persuaded to break off, for fear of pride. Mr. Bray coming, encouraged me to proceed in spite of Satan. I prayed Christ to stand by me, and finished the hymn. Upon my afterwards showing it to Mr. Bray, the devil threw in a fiery dart, suggesting that it was wrong, and I had displeased God.[11]

Wesley was possibly thinking of these circumstances as he was framing the third stanza. He desired to display God's righteousness—that is, to make known to others his extravagant gospel experience—but Satan tried to hinder him. Nevertheless, he wrote in his journal on the same day he devised the hymn:

---

11. Kimbrough and Newport, *Manuscript Journal*, 1:109 (23 May 1738). Mr. Bray was a simple man who served as a spiritual guide to Charles, especially when Charles was sick and struggling spiritually. Charles described him as "a poor, ignorant mechanic, who knows nothing but Christ; yet by knowing him, knows and discerns all things." See also Larrabee, *Wesley and His Coadjutors*, 2:28–29.

> But God has showed me, he can defend me from it, while speaking for him. In his name therefore, and through his strength, I will perform my vows unto the Lord, of not hiding his righteousness within my heart, if it should ever please him to plant it there.[12]

Noticeably, the latter part of this quote and the last two lines of stanza three are identical. This adds evidence to the claim for this being the text Wesley described as the "hymn upon my conversion." Wesley's covenant with God to announce the good news of salvation to others is striking. With the Holy Spirit's help, he kept this vow until his death on March 29, 1788.

STANZA 4

> No, tho' the ancient dragon rage,
>   And call forth all his host[13] to war,
> Tho' earth's self-righteous sons engage,
>   Them and their god alike I dare;
> Jesus, the sinner's friend, proclaim;
> Jesus, to sinners still the same.

In the fourth stanza, Wesley called Satan "the ancient dragon," a metaphor John the Beloved often used to describe Satan in his Revelation. Wesley was aware of the ways the devil tries to hinder sinners from coming to Christ. The "dragon" often whispers in the sinner's ears: "You are too sinful to come to Jesus." But in the fifth line, challenging Satan and "all his host," Wesley proclaimed Jesus as "the sinner's friend." The original title of the hymn, "Christ the Friend of Sinners," was derived from this line. Wesley concluded the stanza by stressing how this beautiful truth is unchanging: "Jesus, to sinners still the same."

STANZA 5

> Outcasts of men, to you I call,
>   Harlots, and publicans, and theives!
> He spreads his arms t' embrace you all;
>   Sinners alone his grace receives.
> No need of him the righteous have;
> He came the lost to seek and save.

---

12. Kimbrough and Newport, *Manuscript Journal*, 1:110 (23 May 1738).
13. hosts : *HSP* (1739).

In the fifth stanza, Wesley began to exhort sinners to come to Christ. He wrote with profound simplicity, yet as one possessed of biblical authority. He called to those of his time who were socially insignificant, the "outcast," who might feel too unworthy to come to Jesus. With an evangelistic zeal, he invited the most morally depraved, the "harlots, and publicans, and thieves!" Wesley assured them, regardless of their social or moral status, Jesus is graciously willing to embrace them all. Why? Because this is why Jesus came—"to seek and save" those who were lost. Clearly, Wesley had Luke 19:10 in mind, but he might also have been thinking of Matthew 9:13, "for I am not come to call the righteous, but sinners to repentance."

STANZA 6

> Come, all ye Magdalens in lust,
>   Ye ruffians fell in murders old;[14]
> Repent, and live; despair, and trust!
>   Jesus for you to death was sold;
> Tho' hell protest and earth repine,
> He died for crimes like yours—and mine.

Stanza six, much like stanza five, calls out to the depraved and invites them to find life in Jesus.

The term "Magdalens," a plural form of "Magdalen" or "Magdalene," refers to Mary, "out of whom went seven devils" (Luke 8:12). It is also commonly attributed to the unnamed woman in Luke 7:36–50 who was called "a sinner." However, by using this title, which has become synonymous with the image of a reformed prostitute, Wesley was emphatically getting the attention of all women who struggle with lust, not just the notoriously immoral. They too must repent of their sins and trust in Jesus for their salvation. Jesus died for them, too. Jesus' death for the wicked makes "hell protest

---

14. Some scholars, including Baker, *Representative Verse*, 4; Lawson, *A Thousand Tongues*, 126; and Maddox, "Hymns and Sacred Poems (1739)," in *Charles Wesley's Published Verse*, 102, assert this line was borrowed from a poem by Samuel Wesley Jr. (1691–1739), "Upon Bishop Atterbury's Birthday," st. 6, l. 2, "The ruffian base, in murder old." Researchers should be aware of the following details: (1) Samuel's poem was not included in his *Poems on Several Occasions* (1736), nor the 2nd ed., posthumous (1743). (2) This poem was included in an 1862 ed., 431–3. In the preface, editor James Nichols indicated the additional texts had been taken from Samuel's MSS. (3) The only known printing in the Wesleys' lifetime was in the *Arminian Magazine* 1 (June 1778) 282–3, unattributed. The resemblance is curious, but quite obscure, and would not have been recognizable to most followers of the Wesleys, except for those close to the Bishop. (4) Samuel's and Charles's text might both allude to an earlier third source, yet undetermined.

and earth repine." But the truth of the matter is Jesus "died for crimes like yours—and mine."

STANZA 7

> Come, O my guilty brethren, come,
> > Groaning beneath your load of sin!
> His bleeding heart shall make you room,
> > His open side shall take you in;
> He calls you now, invites you home—
> Come, O my guilty brethren, come!

In this stanza, Wesley, with evangelistic power, continued to plead to sinners to flee to Jesus. They need to come for forgiveness because they are guilty. He anticipated a possible excuse from his hearers: there is no room for them, perhaps. In response, he confirmed to them Christ's "bleeding heart shall make you room" and "His open side shall take you in." This metaphor is powerful, for it vividly conveys the message that there is always room for us at the cross. In line five, to further persuade his "guilty brethren," he insisted Christ himself was calling them. This is a reflection upon Matthew 11:28, "Come unto me, all ye that labour and are heavy laden, and I will give you rest." Therefore, no one can say, "I am not invited, and thus I cannot come." Furthermore, this universal gospel call stresses the sinner's responsibility to come to Jesus. It also emphasizes the call's urgent nature—all must come now.

STANZA 8

> For you the purple current flowed,
> > In pardons from his wounded side;
> Languished for you th' eternal God;
> > For you the Prince of Glory died;
> Believe, and all your sin's[15] forgiv'n;
> Only believe, and yours is heav'n!

This verse, the hymn's climax, is overtly christological. Wesley portrayed Jesus as "the eternal God," then said, in a striking way, this eternal God "languished," or suffered. We find a similar theme in Wesley's hymn "And can it be," in which he bursts out: "Amazing love! How can it be, that Thou, my God, shouldst die for me?" Certainly, Wesley was not promoting patripassianism,

---

15. guilt's : *HSP* (1739).

which teaches God the Father suffered and died. But then why would he say God suffered? No doubt, he wanted to press upon his readers the paradox of atonement and the unique nature of Jesus as God-man. Since the deity and humanity of Jesus Christ are inseparable, what ultimately caused Wesley to wonder is how the eternal God, the Lord Jesus Christ, would die for such a sinner as he. The frequent use of the phrase "for you"—as in line four: "For you the Prince of glory died"—probably reveals the author's belief in unlimited atonement, one peculiar doctrine of Arminian Methodism with which Calvinist Methodists (like George Whitefield) would not agree. At the same time, for Wesley, Christ's death will not have any effect if sinners do not believe in Jesus. Thus, he asks them to believe and all their sins will be forgiven. But they might say, "Is faith in Christ enough?" Yes, it is. "Only believe, and yours is Heaven," declares the Methodist writer. This is the cardinal Protestant doctrine of justification by faith alone, from which all Wesley's succeeding hymns flow.

CONCLUSION

Have you been redeemed by the blood of Christ? If so, does this doctrine of redemption still cause you to be amazed and thank the triune God for redeeming such worthless slaves as you and me? Do you proclaim this great news of redemption to others who are still children of "wrath and hell"? Where shall our wondering souls begin?[16]

---

16. A version of this article was previously published as "'Where Shall My Wondering Soul Begin?' A historical and theological analysis," *Puritan Reformed Journal* 3/2 (2011) 291–98. Used by permission.

2

And can it be that I should gain

STEVE WEAVER

This hymn is closely associated with Charles Wesley's conversion experience and was probably written soon after. It was first published in *Hymns and Sacred Poems* (1739), where it was titled "Free Grace."[1]

In 1738, when Charles was on the verge of renouncing his works-based faith in favor of the free grace described in this hymn, he had been introduced to Martin Luther's commentary on Galatians. He described the experience in his journal on May 17, 1738:

> Today I first saw Luther on the Galatians, which Mr. [William] Holland had accidentally lit upon. We began, and found him nobly full of faith. My friend, in hearing him, was so affected as to breathe out sighs and groans unutterable. I marveled that we were so soon, and so entirely, removed from him that called us into the grace of Christ unto another gospel. Who would believe our Church had been founded on this important article of justification by faith alone! I am astonished I should ever think this is a new doctrine.... From this time I endeavoured to ground as many of our friends as came in this fundamental truth, salvation by faith alone; not an idle, dead faith, but a faith which works

---

1. The hymn was repeated in *A Collection of Hymns* (1742), *A Collection of Tunes . . . Sung at the Foundery* (1742, first st. only), *Hymns and Sacred Poems* [HSP] (1747), *Hymns for Those to Whom Christ is All in All* [HTWCAA] (1761), and *A Collection of Hymns for the Use of the People Called Methodists* (1780) with different punctuation and the fifth stanza omitted.

> by love, and is necessarily productive of all good works and all holiness.
>
> I spent some hours this evening in private with Martin Luther, who was greatly blessed to me, especially his conclusion of the second chapter. I laboured, waited, and prayed to see "who loved me, and gave himself for me."[2]

Martin Luther's commentary on Galatians 2:20 is especially notable for its apparent influence on Wesley's faith and on his hymn:

> Here have ye the true Manner of Justification set before your eyes, and a perfect example of the assurance of faith. He that can with a firm and constant faith say these words with Paul, "I live by faith in the Son of God, who loved me, and gave himself for me," is happy indeed. . . .
>
> Who is this Me? Even I, wretched and damnable sinner, so dearly beloved of the Son of God, that he gave himself for me. If I then, through the works or merits could have loved the Son of God, and so come unto him, what needed he to deliver himself for me?
>
> Wherefore these words, "which loved me," are full of faith. And he that can utter the word "me," and apply it unto himself with a true and constant faith, as Paul did, shall be a good disputer with Paul against the law; for he delivered neither sheep, ox, gold, nor silver, but even God himself entirely and wholly, for me, even for me (I say) a miserable and a wretched sinner. Now therefore, in that the Son of God was thus delivered to death for me, I take comfort and apply this benefit unto my self. And this manner of applying is the very true force and power of faith.[3]

The opening lines of Wesley's hymn seem to flow naturally in response:

> And can it be that I should gain
>   An int'rest in the Savior's blood?[4]
> Died he for me,[5] who caused his pain!
>   For me![6] who him to death pursued.
> Amazing love! How can it be
> That thou, my God, shouldst die for me?

2. Kimbrough and Newport, *Manuscript Journal*, 1:103–4.

3. Luther, *Commentary Upon Galatians*, 72–73.

4. blood! : *HSP* (1739, 1747), *Collection of Hymns* (1742), *Collection of Tunes* (1742).

5. me?— : *HSP* (1739, 1747), *Collection of Hymns* (1742), *Collection of Tunes* (1742), *HTWCAA* (1761).

6. me?— : *HSP* (1739, 1747), *Collection of Hymns* (1742), *Collection of Tunes* (1742), *HTWCAA* (1761).

Wesley was clearly amazed at the extravagant grace of God evident in his own salvation. He was amazed how this God would have offered his life for him, the sinner responsible for that death penalty. Wesley put himself in the place of the angry crowd, the masses who cried "Crucify him!" and whom Peter indicted on the day of Pentecost (Acts 2:23). This thought caused Wesley to cry out, "Amazing love!" and question, "How can it be / That thou, my God, shouldst die for me?" Wesley's attribution of death to God is at first a shocking statement. He wished it to be so. It is doubtful Wesley was espousing a form of patripassianism in these words. Instead, he wished for those who sing this hymn to understand the amazing love of God, which resulted in the death of the Son of God, the God-man, Jesus Christ. This expression, as used by Wesley, is thoroughly orthodox as it reflects the hypostatic union of the divine and human natures of Jesus. What is said of one nature can be said of the other since the two natures are united in one hypostasis, or person. Scripture also speaks this way of the death of Jesus when the apostle Paul exhorted the Ephesian elders "to care for the church of God, which he obtained with his own blood." (Acts 20:28). Here, the blood of God refers to the blood of Jesus, the God-man.

STANZA 2

> 'Tis myst'ry all:[7] th' Immortal dies!
>   Who can explore his[8] strange design?
> In vain the first-born seraph tries
>   To sound the depths of love divine.
> 'Tis mercy all! Let earth adore;
> Let angel minds inquire no more.

Again in stanza two, Wesley probed the mystery of the death of the Son of God for us. Here Wesley juxtaposed immortality and death. These two obviously do not belong together, but he placed them together to emphasize the mystery of the atonement. The depth of this mystery is highlighted by his speculative description of angelic attempts to understand "the depths of love divine." This is no doubt a reflection upon 1 Peter 1:12, which describes the gospel as "good news . . . into which angels long to look." Wesley was content to put an end to the speculation with the declaration that it is simply a mystery of mercy.

---

    7. all! : *HSP* (1739, 1747), *Collection of Hymns* (1742).
    8. this : *Collection*, 7th ed. (1791).

STANZA 3

> He left his Father's throne above,
>   (So free, so infinite His grace![9])
> Emptied himself of all but love,
>   And bled for Adam's helpless race:
> 'Tis mercy all, immense and free,[10]
> For O my God,[11] it found out me!

In the third stanza, Wesley explored the kenosis or "self-emptying" of Christ in the Incarnation. The amazing love of God is seen in the way it caused the Son to leave "His Father's throne above." This demonstrates the freeness and infinite nature of his grace. Philippians 2:5–8 seems to be the scriptural backdrop for this stanza. These verses describe the depths to which the Son had descended in the Incarnation. Wesley revealed an understanding of the underlying Greek of Philippians 2:7—the Greek word *ekenosen* means "he emptied himself," which Wesley used here, as opposed to the King James Version, which uses the phrase "made himself of no reputation." The climax of the Incarnation, however, is seen in the hymn in Christ's death on the cross (as it is in Philippians 2:8). He "bled for Adam's helpless race." Again, the hymnist is forced to confess how the mercy of God alone is the source of this amazing love. The personal nature of Wesleyan evangelism is seen in the use of "me" throughout the hymn. The notion Christ died "for me" is repeated three times in the first stanza, and in this third stanza the mercy of God is said to have "found out me!" This personal emphasis is even more evident in stanzas four through six.

STANZA 4

> Long my imprisoned spirit lay,
>   Fast bound in sin and nature's night;
> Thine eye diffused a quick'ning ray;
>   I woke; the dungeon flamed with light![12]
> My chains fell off, my heart was free,
> I rose, went forth, and followed Thee.

---

9. grace : *HTWCAA* (1761).

10. free! : *HSP* (1739, 1747), *Collection of Hymns* (1742).

11. God! : *HSP* (1739), *Collection of Hymns* (1742).

12. light;: *HSP* (1739, 1747), *Collection of Hymns* (1742), *HTWCAA* (1761), *Collection*, eds. 1–2 (1780–1781).

In the final three stanzas, Wesley seemed to offer his own testimony from his experience of conversion. It is important to note how the language is not just profoundly personal, it is also deeply biblical and theological. Wesley's view of his pre-conversion state was that of an "imprisoned spirit" bound by both sin and nature. Wesley drew on the imagery of a prisoner bound by chains in a dungeon. This is an apt image of the state of mankind as described in Ephesians 2:1–3:

> And you were dead in the trespasses and sins in which you once walked, following the course of this world, following the prince of the power of the air, the spirit that is now at work in the sons of disobedience—among whom we all once lived in the passions of our flesh, carrying out the desires of the body and the mind, and were by nature children of wrath, like the rest of mankind (ESV).

This picture of mankind as dead in "trespasses and sins" and "by nature children of wrath" could be the source for Wesley's "fast bound in sin and nature's might." In the next line, Wesley described "a quickening ray" emitted from the eye of God, which caused Wesley to awaken from his slumber of sin and death. The language of quickening or "making alive" is present in the King James Version of Ephesians 2:1 and 4: "And you hath he quickened, who were dead in trespasses and sins; . . . Even when we were dead in sins, hath quickened us together with Christ." The quickening of the sinner resulted in a dungeon now inflamed with light, chains being broken, and a heart set free. Wesley's response to the quickening work of God was to rise up and follow Christ. This combination of the biblical images of life, light, freedom from sin, and freedom of heart testify to a profound understanding of the transformation that takes place at regeneration.

STANZA 5

> Still the small inward voice I hear
>   That whispers all my sins forgiv'n;
> Still th' atoning blood is near,
>   That quenched the wrath of hostile Heav'n.
> I feel the life his wounds impart;
> I feel my Saviour in my heart.

Before Wesley's conversion, he longed for assurance of forgiveness. This assurance came in the presence of the Holy Spirit. There might be an allusion to the inward witness of the Spirit in 1 John 5:10, but the event Wesley has expressed here is largely experiential. The "small inward voice . . . whispers all my sins forgiven." Even so, the true basis for this event is the objective work of Christ on the cross. It was Jesus' "atoning blood" which "quenched the wrath of hostile heaven." This vivid imagery of the death of Christ satisfying the wrath of a holy God is seen in the Scripture's use of the word "propitiation" in Romans 3:25, 1 John 2:2, and 1 John 4:10. The word "propitiation" means "to satisfy wrath." Christ on the cross propitiated a holy God on our behalf.

STANZA 6

> No condemnation now I dread;
>   Jesus, and all in him, is mine;
> Alive in him, my living Head,
>   And clothed in righteousness divine,
> Bold I approach th' eternal throne,
> And claim the crown, through Christ, my own.

Wesley began his final stanza with words reflecting Romans 8:1, "There is therefore now no condemnation for them which are in Christ Jesus" (KJV). These hope-filled words provide an opportunity for reflection upon the imputation of Christ's righteousness in justification. The believer need not fear God's condemnation, because we are united to Jesus Christ through faith: "Jesus, and all in Him, is mine." This includes Christ's righteousness, as Wesley specified how the now-alive sinner is "clothed in righteousness divine." This evokes biblical imagery from Genesis 3, when God provided coats of skin to cover the nakedness of Adam and Eve, and Zechariah 3, when God provided a change of raiment for the dirty clothes of Joshua the high priest. These words also reflect a careful reading of 2 Corinthians 5:21, which states, "For he [God] hath made him [Jesus] to be sin for us, who knew no sin; that we might be made the righteousness of God in him." On the basis of this clothing with the righteousness of Christ, we are enabled to approach "th' eternal throne" boldly.

Also alluded to here is the work of Jesus, our great High Priest (Heb 4:16), which allows the author to exhort his readers, "Let us therefore come boldly unto the throne of grace, that we may obtain mercy, and find grace to help in time of need." Wesley closed the hymn with the phrase "through Christ my own." This is an apt summary of the hymn's teaching and of Wesley's theology. All our blessings are through Christ (the objective work of Christ) and are ours by faith (the experiential possession).

Because of its rich doctrinal and devotional quality, it is no wonder this hymn has stood the test of time and remains a favorite of congregations in the twenty-first century. The enduring relevance of this hymn was brought home to me in recent years at Together for the Gospel conferences, when crowds of several thousand people sang this hymn with deep affection at the tops of their lungs. Tears streamed down their faces, and arms were uplifted as they sang of the amazing love of God, as seen in the death of Christ for their sins.

3

O for a thousand tongues to sing

JONATHAN A. POWERS

It is a bold yet defendable claim to state that no corpus of song better exemplifies the proclamation of the gospel in lyrical form than the hymnody of Charles Wesley. Undoubtedly, Wesley's keen ability as a wordsmith to craft rich theological poetry, filled with scriptural imagery, affectionate expression, and doxological testimony to the "Gospel-Word," has set him apart as one of the most dynamic and well-beloved hymnwriters of the past three centuries.[1] The message of salvation through Christ was paramount in Wesley's ministry and lyrical thought.[2] Continually in his hymns Wesley testified to the divine love and grace of God, which is powerful enough to convert any individual from a life of sin to a life of holy love.

One striking feature of Wesley's lyricism is his emphasis on the extent of God's saving work. He claimed this is not only powerful enough to save from future perdition but also to save "to the uttermost" in the here-and-now by leading toward Christian perfection.[3] This active soteriology was foundational

---

1. Charles Wesley often referred to the work of Christ as the "Gospel-Word" in his hymns. For example, see the hymn "Sinners obey the Gospel Word," from *Hymns on the Great Festivals* (1746) 44–46, available online via Hymnology Archive, ed. Chris Fenner, https://www.hymnologyarchive.com/charles-john-wesley-works, or Charles Wesley's Published Verse, ed. Randy L. Maddox, https://divinity.duke.edu/initiatives/cswt/charles-published-verse

2. For an essay on the pervasive focus on salvation in Charles Wesley's works, see Tyson, "I Preached the Cross," 204–28.

3. See especially "And are we yet alive," in *Hymns and Sacred Poems* (1749) 2:321–2.

in both John and Charles Wesley's thought as they established the early Methodist societies. The themes of God's free grace and invitation to full salvation were central in the doctrines of the early Methodist movement, providing it with a dynamic evangelistic impulse and distinct message. Given such strong soteriological emphasis, it is no surprise, then, how a considerable number of Charles Wesley's hymns address the experience of Christian salvation, made possible by the justifying work of Jesus Christ and the sanctifying power of the Holy Spirit.[4] Within Wesley's hymnody is an obvious soteriological tapestry, bearing witness to God's saving grace through Jesus Christ.

Another distinct characteristic of Wesley's lyricism is how his hymns maintain a God-oriented, doxological focus while declaring the message of salvation in a very personal and applicable manner. To put it another way, Wesley's hymns simultaneously hold together doxology, testimony, and evangelism as they announce with bold proclamation and praise the redemptive power of God made available to every individual. Wesley had a unique way of giving praise to God while still using his lyrics to exhort others to accept the Gospel for themselves. Considering the *kerygmatic* quality of his hymns, then, Wesley's model is one of doxology, testimony, proclamation, and exhortation.[5]

A significant and popular hymn in which Wesley's kerygmatic model is easily discerned is "For the Anniversary Day of One's Conversion," more commonly known today as "O for a thousand tongues to sing." As the original title of the work indicates, Charles Wesley wrote the hymn on the one-year anniversary of his conversion experience, Pentecost Sunday, May 21, 1738.

It is fitting how Charles Wesley's experiential assurance of Christ's love and forgiveness occurred on a Pentecost Sunday. This personal Pentecost for Charles came during a time of deep searching for the assurance of Christ's presence and protection. Following a brief stint of missionary-work in the Americas, Wesley returned to England, due in part to severe illness.[6] Throughout the spring of 1738, he was severely troubled by both his illness and his disappointment in not being able to continue his missionary work. While battling what was most likely pneumonia, Wesley moved into the home of his friend John Bray on May 11, 1738.[7] Wesley stayed with Bray

---

4. See Newton, "Brothers in Arms," 62–3.

5. The term *kerygma* is an ancient Greek word for preaching.

6. In the spring of 1738, Charles wrote to his brother Samuel: "One consequence of my sickness you will not be sorry for, stopping my sudden return to Georgia. For the doctors tell me to undertake a voyage now would be certain death." See Newport and Lloyd, *Letters of Charles Wesley,* 1:67–68.

7. For this and the following quotes from Wesley's journal, see Kimbrough and Newport, *Manuscript Journal.* In his journal entry for 11 May 1738, Wesley called John

as he recovered from his illness, using the time for prayer and earnest conversation with friends on topics of death, forgiveness, and the atoning work of God. Biographer John Tyson noted how Wesley's stay in the Bray home served as a spiritual retreat of sorts, allowing Charles the space to grapple with intense physical and spiritual health while seeking a deeper knowledge of God's atoning work in his life.[8]

Charles's journal entries during his stay at the Bray house reveal the ever-shifting nature of his spiritual state and his deep longing within to truly know God's saving grace. For example, Charles noted in his entry on May 16, 1738: "Waked weary, faithless, and heartless. . . . In the afternoon I seemed deeply sensible of my misery, in being without Christ." The following day, Wesley mentioned how his friend William Holland stopped by to read Martin Luther's *Galatians* with him, and both he and Mr. Holland were deeply moved by Luther's insights on the doctrine of justification by faith. This entry seems to indicate some sort of resolve in his spirit, yet it was short lived, as another shift is seen in his writing on May 19: "At five this morning the pain and difficulty in breathing returned. . . . Not much desire. Received the Sacrament, but not Christ." Then again on May 20: "I waked much disappointed, and continued all day in great dejection, which the Sacrament did not in the least abate. Nevertheless God would not suffer me to doubt the truth of his promises."

On Sunday, May 21, Charles finally received the assurance he sought. That morning, John stopped by along with some friends for a visit. Being Pentecost, they sang a song to the Holy Ghost before departing, leaving Charles in prayer for God to send the Holy Spirit as comforter in his own life. Later that day, Charles turned to his Bible, seeking words of consolation. His eye fell upon Isaiah 40:1: "Comfort ye, comfort ye, my people, saith your God: speak ye comfortably to Jerusalem, and cry unto her that her warfare is accomplished, that her iniquity is pardoned, for she had received the Lord's hand double of all her sin" (KJV). After reading these verses, Charles wrote the following in his journal:

> I now found myself at peace with God, and rejoiced in the hope of loving Christ. My temper for the rest of the day was mistrust of my own great, but before unknown, weakness. I saw that by faith I stood; by the continual support of faith, which kept me from falling, though of myself I am ever sinking into sin. I went

---

Bray "a poor, ignorant mechanic, who knows nothing but Christ; yet by knowing him, knows and discerns all things."

8. Tyson, *Assist Me to Proclaim*, 44.

to bed still sensible of my own weakness (I humbly hope to be more and more so), yet confident of Christ's protection.

Knowing by faith in Jesus Christ his sins were truly forgiven and he was set free from their bondage, Charles was assured of God's saving grace at work in his life. From this time forward, an obvious shift occured in the content of his journals, showing he had truly found peace with God.

John R. Tyson identified Wesley's assurance experience as a "personal Pentecost,"[9] a fitting classification beyond the obvious reason the event occurred on Pentecost Sunday. For one, similar to those gathered in the upper room on Pentecost, Charles Wesley's experience included a filling of the Spirit, whereby he received the assurance of Christ's saving and empowering work. Moreover, Wesley's personal Pentecost resulted in his tongue (i.e. pen) being set free for proclamation of God's Word. Wesley's encounter with God's saving grace opened a doorway to a new world of lyrical expression in his preaching and in his hymn writing. To be sure, reflection through poetic form was a familiar practice for Wesley; Charles had been an avid poet since his childhood. Combining his poetic skill with the experience of God's salvation, however, Wesley began to proclaim God's message with new vigor, placing emphasis on the power of Christ for salvation within his lyrical verse. As Tyson pointed out, "The bondage to sin and the darkness of doubt had been broken and driven away when Christ came into the poet's life. Charles Wesley used images of manumission and liberation to communicate the freedom that he now felt because of his faith in Christ."[10]

Charles composed the hymn "O for a thousand tongues to sing" on the one-year anniversary of his personal Pentecost. It was published the following year in *Hymns and Sacred Poems* (1740), in eighteen stanzas, originally beginning "Glory to God, and praise, and love."[11] Curiously, Charles did not mark this anniversary in his journal. He only briefly mentioned a gathering at the home of Metcalf Claggett, together with several other friends, including George Whitefield and John Cennick. Nonetheless, he did remember the day of his conversion throughout his life; he mentioned it in a letter to his wife on Whitsunday, 1760:

---

9. Tyson, *Assist Me to Proclaim*, 40.

10. Tyson, *Assist Me to Proclaim*, 50.

11. The hymn was reduced to eleven stanzas, beginning "O for a thousand tongues to sing," in *Hymns and Spiritual Songs* (1753), using sts. 7–13, 15–18. In the *Collection of Hymns* (1780), it was further reduced to nine stanzas, using sts. 7–10, 12–14, 17–18; this selection was repeated in the second *Pocket Hymn Book* (1787). Italics given here as in the 1740 version.

> This I once called the anniversary of my conversion. Just twenty-two years ago I thought I received the first grain of faith. But what does that avail me, if I have not the Spirit now? "I account that the long-suffering of the Lord is salvation," and would fain believe He has reserved me so long for good, and not for evil.[12]

His anniversary hymn stands as a reflection of his own inner experience of salvation, giving testimonial praise to the work of Jesus Christ while exhorting others to personally accept the saving work of God. The hymn begins with an opening doxology, calling heaven and earth—the church triumphant, the church militant, and all the communion of saints—to join in praise:

> Glory to God, and praise, and love
>   Be ever, ever giv'n;
> By saints below, and saints above,
>   The church in earth and heav'n.

The hymn then hones in, moving from grand cosmic doxology to particular testimony of God's work. Here, Charles got personal, giving testimonial account to the peace and assurance he found in his personal Pentecost:

> On this glad day the glorious Sun
>   Of Righteousness arose;
> On my benighted soul he shone
>   And filled it with repose.
>
> Sudden expired the legal strife;
>   'Twas then I ceased to grieve;
> My second, real, living life
>   I then began to live.
>
> Then with my heart I first believed,
>   Believed, with faith divine,
> Power with the Holy Ghost received
>   To call the Savior *mine*.
>
> I felt my Lord's atoning blood
>   Close to my soul applied;
> *Me, me* he loved—the Son of God,
>   For *me*, for *me* he died!
>
> I found and owned his promise true,
>   Ascertained of *my* part,

---

12. Tyson, *Charles Wesley: A Reader*, 110.

> My pardon passed in heav'en I *knew*
> When written on my heart.

In the above lyrics, the Wesley himself was the primary subject. This was his testimony of God's saving grace, using language reflective of his journal entries on May 21 and 22, 1738. The parallel is especially seen in the following lines: "On this glad day the glorious Sun / of Righteousness arose; / on my benighted soul he shone / and filled it with repose," and "Me, me he loved, the Son of God, / for me, for me he died!" While his lyrics here undoubtedly give personal witness to God's work in his life, they also invite singers and readers to make their own personal connections to Charles's experience. Wesley claimed salvation occurs solely because of the work of God, yet he also emphasized salvation can be claimed as one's own. Charles made an important declaration here in the way every Christian testimony witnesses to the work of God, whose salvation is free and available for all to claim.

Following his testimonial declaration, stanzas seven and eight set up an important lyrical shift in the song. Here, he showed how personal assurance of God's work in one's life (his own in particular) gives way to a desire for Gospel proclamation. He began by offering a prayer for God to empower and "assist" in such a proclamation:

> O for a thousand tongues to sing[13]
> My dear Redeemer's praise!
> The glories of my God and King,
> The triumphs of his grace.
>
> My gracious Master, and my God,
> Assist me to proclaim,
> To spread through all the earth abroad
> The honors of thy name.

In the seventh stanza, Charles made a personal appeal for "a thousand tongues" to proclaim their praise to God, desiring with robust vigor to acknowledge God's glories and triumphs. Stanza eight continues the prayer with his request for assistance in using the tongue he has been given by God to spread the good news of Jesus Christ.[14] Stanzas nine through eleven then convey his sermon-in-rhyme:

---

13. "'O for a thousand tongues to sing' is supposed to have had its origin in an expression of Peter Böhler, the Moravian, who, when consulted by C. Wesley about praising Christ, replied, 'Had I a thousand tongues, I would praise Him with them all.'" Julian, *Dictionary of Hymnology*, 428.

14. It is a gripping thought to realize that by the church's joining Charles in singing this hymn throughout the years, in a sense God has granted Charles the thousand

> Jesus, the name that charms our fears,
> > That bids our sorrows cease;
> 'Tis music in the sinner's ears,
> > 'Tis life, and health, and peace!
>
> He breaks the power of cancelled sin,
> > He sets the prisoner free;
> His blood can make the foulest clean,
> > His blood availed for me.
>
> He speaks, and listening to his voice,
> > New life the dead receive;
> The mournful, broken hearts rejoice,
> > The humble poor *believe*.

Wesley's kerygmatic emphasis is evident in the above stanzas. In the lyrics, Charles proclaimed the power and work of Jesus Christ while noting its unlimited application. For instance, stanzas ten and eleven show Christ's salvation at work in specific experiences of those to whom the proclamation is addressed: sinners are freed from the power of sin; prisoners are set free; the dead are given life; the sorrowful are given joy. In naming these particular circumstances, Wesley acknowledged how Christ's work is offered to all and has the power to reach into and redeem any particular circumstance. For Wesley, God's unlimited grace is the beauty of the Gospel.

This particularized and personalized lyrical focus continues in the final seven stanzas of the hymn, only in a new direction. Having given praise to God, testimony to God's work, and declaration of the Gospel, Wesley then boldly commanded others to make the Gospel their own, to accept the triumphs of Christ, and to join in doxological proclamation. While the emphasis was implicit earlier in the song, the hymn concludes with an explicit exhortation for all to personally experience Jesus, the one who redeems, heals, and shows the way of true, heavenly love:

> Hear him ye deaf, his praise, ye dumb,
> > Your loosened tongues employ;
> Ye blind, behold your Savior come,
> > And leap, ye lame, for joy.
>
> Look unto him, ye nations, own
> > Your God, ye fallen race!
> Look, and be saved, through faith alone;
> > Be justified by grace!

---

tongues he so desired to proclaim God's praise.

See all your sins on Jesus laid;
    The Lamb of God was slain;
His soul was once an offering made
    For *every soul* of man.

Harlots, and publicans, and thieves,
    In holy triumph join!
Saved is the sinner that believes
    From crimes as great as mine.

Murd'rers and all ye hellish crew,
    Ye sons of lust and pride,[15]
Believe the Savior died for you;
    For me[16] the Savior died.

Awake from guilty nature's sleep,
    And Christ shall give you light;
Cast all your sins into the deep,
    And wash the Ethiop white.[17]

With me, your chief, you[18] then shall *know*,
    Shall feel your sins forgiv'n,
Anticipate your heav'n below,
    And own that love is heav'n.

From beginning to end, the personal experience of Christ's salvation is held in high significance in this hymn. This emphasis on personal experience in Wesley's hymnody is important and needs brief examination. Wesley never denied experience as a convincing indicator of a personal faith, yet he understood experience as the inner witness of the Holy Spirit at work in a person's life.[19] One way the inner witness of faith was manifest in believers was when they joined together to proclaim praise to God for his justifying and sanctifying grace, which is precisely why Wesley labored so extensively

---

15. Blackened with lust and pride : *HSS*, eds. 1–21, 23 (1753–1777, 1782).

16. you : *HSS*, all eds. (1753–1786).

17. This line is properly omitted from modern hymnals for its proposal of lightening an African's skin color. The stanza can be retained for modern use by replacing "the Ethiop" with a non-racial term, such as "our garments" or "the darkness," to be consistent with the image of washing in Revelation 7:14.

18. ye : *HSS*, all eds. (1753–1786); *Collection*, eds. 1–6 (1780–1788); *Pocket Hymn Book* (1787).

19. For example, see stanza four of the hymn.

to provide hymns for the early Methodists to declare their faith and love of God corporately.

Experience, in Wesleyan thought, serves as confirmation of the gospel at work in an individual's life. While it is never meant to be elevated to an authority all its own, it does affirm knowledge of salvation in a deeply personal and affectionate way. It is thus fitting in the way Charles's hymns (like "O for a thousand tongues to sing") are saturated with affectionate language, and in the way he so intensely emphasized the personal experience of salvation. The doxological and theological richness of his hymns reflects his ardent belief in the way the inner experience of salvation is manifest through outward proclamation. Though many may not feel as gifted in songwriting as Charles Wesley, every Christian has a message to proclaim. As Charles has brilliantly demonstrated in this hymn, all Christian testimony witnesses to God, tells the story of salvation, proclaims the gospel message, and encourages others toward a saving knowledge of Jesus Christ. May God assist our tongues as we boldly declare our Savior's praise.

Struggle & Respite

4

Jesu, lover of my soul

PATRICK A. EBY & CHRISTOPHER P. MCFADDEN

In Temptation

Jesu, lover of my soul,[1]
    Let me to thy bosom fly,
While the nearer waters roll,
    While the tempest still is high;
Hide me, O my Saviour, hide,
    Till the storm of life is past;
Safe into the haven guide;
    O receive my soul at last.

Other refuge have I none;
    Hangs my helpless soul on thee;
Leave, ah! Leave me not alone,
    Still support and comfort me.
All my trust on thee is stay'd;
    All my help from thee I bring;

---

1. Some scholars believe this first line (and perhaps the broader theme of the hymn) was inspired by the Wisdom of Solomon (Apocrypha) 11:25-26: "And how could any thing have endured, if it had not been thy will? or been preserved, if not called by thee? But thou sparest all: for they are thine, O Lord, thou lover of souls" (KJV). For an examination of the Wesleyan use of the Apocrypha, see Charlesworth, *Proceedings of the Charles Wesley Society*, 3:63–88. See also the exhaustive "Scriptural Index to the Poetry of Charles Wesley" compiled by S.T. Kimbrough in *Lyrical Theology*, 297–381, in which it appears Charles never used an apocryphal book as the stated basis for a hymn.

> Cover my defenceless head
>   With the shadow of thy wing.
>
> Wilt thou not regard my call?
>   Wilt thou not accept my prayer?
> Lo! I sink, I faint, I fall—
>   Lo! On thee I cast my care;
> Reach me out thy gracious hand!
>   While I of thy strength receive,
> Hoping against hope I stand,
>   Dying, and behold I live!
>
> Thou, O Christ, art all I want,
>   More than all in thee I find;
> Raise the fallen, cheer the faint,
>   Heal the sick, and lead the blind;
> Just and holy is thy name;
>   I am all unrighteousness;
> False, and full of sin I am;
>   Thou art full of truth and grace.
>
> Plenteous grace with thee is found,
>   Grace to cover all my sin;
> Let the healing streams abound;
>   Make and keep me pure within;
> Thou of life the fountain art;
>   Freely let me take of thee;
> Spring thou up within my heart;
>   Rise to all eternity!

"Jesu, lover of my soul" was published four times during Charles Wesley's life. It was included in its entirety in *Hymns and Sacred Poems* (1740) and the *Pocket Hymn Book* (1785). What seems to be the turning point and the focus of the hymn is stanza three, which was left out of *Hymns and Spiritual Songs* (1753) and *Select Hymns* (1765). The shortened version (without stanza three) is most often copied in later hymnals. This has been one of Charles's most enduring and popular hymns.

PRAYERS IN THE STORM

One of the gifts Charles Wesley gave us is a set of tools to examine and explore the tensions of our lives. Sometimes this tension is between two theological positions, but more often it is the tension of living out the Christian faith in times of struggle or temptation. In "Jesu, lover of my soul," Charles explored the struggle of being helpless. He expressed this helplessness through a series of evocative images which highlight both his hopes and his fears. The first part of the hymn uses three images to develop this tension: a storm, a place of refuge, and the refuge of God's wings.

The first image Charles used to describe temptation was a storm. The images and the emotions expressed in this struggle likely flow, at least in part, from his trips across the Atlantic when his ship was tossed about in various storms and he feared for his life. In his journal he described several tempests, but one in particular was described in vivid detail, on October 28, 1736:

> The captain warned me of a storm approaching. In the evening, at eight, it came, and rose higher and higher, after I thought it must have come to its height. For I did not lose a moment of it, being obliged by the return of my flux to rise continually. At last the long-wished for morning came, and brought no abatement of the storm. There was so prodigious a sea, that it quickly washed away our sheep and half our hogs, and drowned most of our fowl. The ship had been new caulked at Boston; how carefully, it now appeared—for being deeply laden, the sea streamed in at the sides so plentifully, that it was as much as four men could do, by continually pumping, to keep her above water. I rose and lay down by turns, but could remain in no posture long; strove vehemently to pray, but in vain, persisted in striving yet still without effect. I prayed for power to pray, for faith in Jesus Christ, continually repeating his name, till I felt the virtue of it at last, and knew that I abode under the shadow of the Almighty.
>
> It was now about three in the afternoon and the storm at the height I endeavoured to encourage poor Mr. Bridge and Cutler, who were in the utmost agony of fear. I prayed with them, and for them till four, at which time the ship made so much water that the captain, finding it otherwise impossible to save her from sinking, cut down the mizen-mast. In this dreadful moment, I bless God, I found the comfort of hope—and such joy in finding I could hope, as the world can neither give nor take away. I had that conviction of the power of God present with me, overruling my strongest passion, fear, and raising me above what I am by nature, as surpassed all rational evidence, and gave me a taste of the divine goodness. . . .
>
> The wind was still as high as ever but the motion rather less violent since the cutting of the mast, and we did not ship quite so much water. I laid me down, utterly exhausted, but

my distemper was so increased it would not suffer me to rest. Toward morning the sea heard and obeyed the divine voice, "Peace, be still!"[2]

The powerful actor within the storm was water. Water has a multifaceted role in Scripture. On one hand, water is chaotic and unpredictable. The Spirit of God brooded over the water at creation (Gen 1:2). God's treatise on ocean-making in Job indicates how the sea and its waves are "proud" things, but God has mastered them, saying, "This far you may come and no farther" (Job 38:8–11). Charles addressed the present danger of water, but later in the hymn he argued for the life-giving aspect of water. He highlighted the role of the imposing waves in verse 1: "While the nearer waters roll, / While the tempest still is high." The "nearer" waters here are dangerous and life threatening. Perhaps he also had in mind the raw emotions of the disciples sailing during a rolling storm on the sea of Galilee (Matt 8), or God's promise of protection through overwhelming waters and rivers (Isa 43:2).

Charles's description of the storm might also have a double meaning. Is the storm a particular instance in our lives, or is it life itself? The latter is hinted in the phrase, "Safe into the haven guide; / O receive my soul at last." Charles wrote for people who see the storm and feel helpless and defenseless. He expressed the fear of being abandoned by Jesus in the midst of the storm, a thought reinforced at the beginning of stanza three: "Leave, ah! Leave me not alone, / Still support and comfort me." What he desired was a refuge. He longed for comfort and support.

Throughout stanzas one and two Charles appealed to God for rescue; he cried to God for refuge. He wrote, "Hide me, O my Saviour, hide," and "Other refuge have I none," indicating his desperate desire for God's immediate action. Perhaps he recalled God hiding Moses in the cleft of the rock and the safety it supplied (Exod 33:22). This concept of refuge seems taken directly from the Psalms and reflects Charles's mastery of the psalmist's lament (Ps 5:11, 9:9–10, 46:1).

This place of refuge is also described as being covered in the shadow of God's wings ("Cover my defenceless head, / With the shadow of thy wing"). The provision of God is often described powerfully in the Scripture through the metaphor of wings (Ps 17:8, 91:4). It is also possible Charles was drawing on Ruth's prayer, which identifies God's wings with shelter (Ruth 2:12).

Although at the end of stanza two he expressed his trust in God, in stanza three he returned to the doubts he had in the midst of the storm. He was still struggling to have faith in the midst of his doubt. In the first half of

---

2. Kimbrough and Newport, *Manuscript Journal*, 60–61.

stanza three he cried, "Wilt thou not regard my call? / Wilt thou not accept my prayer?" His fear of being left alone in the storm was captured in his pleas for an answer to his prayer. At this point of questioning, he expressed his descent into hopelessness ("Lo! I sink, I faint, I fall—"). Some of the doubt he expressed here resulted from the storm, but equally concerning for Charles was the possibility of unanswered prayer. Again, he evoked the peril at hand; waves threatened to sink him, destroy him, and ultimately lay him low in the grave.

CHARLES'S PENTECOST

As noted above, stanza three seems to be the turning point of the hymn. Here, Charles reached his lowest point, his most desperate moment. The stanza begins with the strongest expression of doubt in the whole hymn. At the beginning of stanza three he wondered if God would hear his call or accept his prayer. If this hymn is a reflection of his life and beliefs, this stanza describes the change Charles experienced in his "personal Pentecost." Before May 21, 1738, Charles was trying to earn the approval and favor of God. He was striving to earn God's acceptance. In this hymn, he personalized this struggle with his use of "I." In the third line of stanza three Charles used "I" to describe his descent. He used "I" again in stanza four when he declared his unrighteousness; he was unworthy of God's healing and grace.

Nonetheless, Charles experienced a breakthrough. Only at his lowest point was he able to accept the work of God in his life. Instead of trying to earn God's favor, Charles said, "Lo! I sink, I faint, I fall— / Lo! On thee I cast my care; / Reach me out thy gracious hand!" Charles probably had in mind Peter's failed attempt to walk on water:

> But when he saw the wind boisterous, he was afraid; and beginning to sink, he cried, saying, "Lord, save me." And immediately Jesus stretched forth his hand, and caught him, and said unto him, "O thou of little faith, wherefore didst thou doubt?" (Matt 14:30–31, KJV).

In this stanza, he illustrated the doctrine of justification by faith through grace alone; he was moved from trying to earn God's favor to accepting God's gracious offer of help. Then he prayed for God to reach out his gracious hand to give him strength; he was relying on God to act, for God to offer the gift of relationship as symbolized in an outstretched hand. The image is of a father who offers his hand to his child for safety and comfort, a hand offered not because the child deserves it, but because the father loves the child.

At the end of stanza three, Charles began a new thread to describe his breakthrough as a resurrection from death to life. The fear expressed in the storm was diminishing as the threat of death was lessened through the promise of life in God. Now he could stand in hope; although he was dying to self he would truly live (Gal 2:20). The seeds of hope here are sown in "truth and grace," indeed, "plenteous grace" (Rom 5:20, 1 Tim 1:14). Charles now prayed because he had received God's grace, instead of his former practice to pray to acquire God's favor. He prayed now with the promise of eternal life. He returned to the resurrection at the end of stanza five.

CONFIDENT PRAYERS

Within this framework of grace and resurrection, there is another change in the language of the hymn. Charles moved from seeing God as a judge to a lover of souls. This changes the language with which Charles talks about Christ. It is a subtle shift, but in stanza two, his expressions of trust and desire for help are for the things Christ can give us, and the ways Christ can support us in our journey. In stanza four, Christ himself is now the center of his desire, not the things Christ can give. He began by saying Christ was all he wanted, then added he could find all he needed in Christ. Because of this new relationship with Christ, Charles was energized to take the message of Christ's love to the world. The next two lines are the only two lines moving from a personal reflection to a general proclamation of God's grace: "Raise the fallen, cheer the faint, / Heal the sick, and lead the blind." This proclamation of the gospel is largely a result of Charles's deeply personal chronicle of his spiritual struggle. The beauty of the hymn is in the way Charles's struggle appeals to us in our shared experience of walking through difficult times with faith in Christ.

After this general proclamation, Charles moved to the heart of the gospel. He contrasted the holiness of God with our unrighteousness and sin. He used an ABBA structure to emphasize the ability of God's holiness, truth, and grace to convert us from our unrighteousness and sin. God's grace is plenteous and is able to cover all our sin. The difference in tone between the first two stanzas and the last two are his assurance. As previously mentioned, in the first half of the hymn, Charles seemed unsure his prayers would be heard, let alone be answered. In stanzas four and five, he spoke confidently of an assurance, despite his own shortcomings.

Charles started this poem with the image of dangerous waters, with the tempest rolling high. At the end of the poem he returned to the image of water, but this time the water heals and gives life (Rev 21:6). This time the waters make and keep us pure. Not only does God cover our sin but he keeps us from sinning. From where do these healing waters come? They come from Christ, who is the fountain of life. As we drink from that fountain, we allow Christ to spring up in our heart.

In stanza five, Charles returned to the image of the resurrection he hinted at in verse three. The result of drinking from the fountain of life is that we rise to all eternity! In stanza three, Charles alluded to Paul's picture of water baptism (Rom 6:4–8). The death we experience in fainting, sinking, falling—in the letting go of our anxieties and our fears in the storm of life—is transformed into new life with Jesus. In stanza three, resurrection impacted the way we live here and now. In stanza five, Charles ended the poem by pointing to a resurrection lasting through all eternity.

CONCLUSION

In this hymn, Charles Wesley detailed his struggle to trust God in the midst of the storm. He began by hinting at his hope: Jesus loves us and will comfort us. At the beginning of the hymn he pleaded for help, but these pleas were colored with doubt. In stanza three, he had a breakthrough. He expressed an assurance in the providence of Christ to reach out his hand and save him. This is a message he was excited to share with all people.

This pattern will potentially repeat in our lives each time we face a new storm. With each new death, each new pain, each new struggle, the grief might lead us to a place of doubt, and yet we can find comfort in knowing we are not alone. It would be nice to think that once we have experienced Christ's love in such a powerful way, our doubts would disappear, but this does not seem to be the way life works. With each new struggle, we might start with our doubts and our fears. But hopefully we move to assurance and acceptance more quickly as we learn to trust in the love of our Savior, who is there with us in the storm.

5

Come, O thou traveller unknown

(Wrestling Jacob)

C. Michael Hawn

> Come, O thou traveller unknown,
>   Whom still I hold, but cannot see;
> My company before is gone,
>   And I am left alone with thee;
> With thee all night I mean to stay,
>   And wrestle till the break of day.

The intercessions, though regretfully often omitted in United Methodist worship, are among the most important parts of the gathered body of Christ. Perhaps the most significant words many parishioners may hear in gathered worship is the absolution: "In the name of Jesus Christ, you are forgiven!" Charles Wesley's hymn "Come, O thou traveller" captures the pure joy of this moment of forgiveness perhaps unlike any other hymn in the English language.

Of the eighteenth-century hymn writers whose hymns are still being sung in the twenty-first century, only Isaac Watts (1674–1748) rivals Charles Wesley in representation in modern hymnals. Because of its Wesleyan roots, *The United Methodist Hymnal* (1989) contains more than twice as many hymns by Wesley than Watts. As we shall see, this hymn ranked very high in the evaluation of Watts, who was largely responsible for liberating English hymnody from the rigid stranglehold of metrical psalmody.[1]

Though it might not be familiar to many readers, "Come, O thou traveller unknown" is one of the most important and, many say, the best of Charles Wesley's hymns. First published in *Hymns and Sacred Poems* (1742) in fourteen stanzas of six lines, under the title "Wrestling Jacob," the hymn is a personal interpretation of the story of Jacob wrestling with the angel of God at Peniel (Gen 32:24–32).[2] At the end of the struggle, Jacob received a new name, Israel. As in any Wesley hymn, poetic verse and Scripture are intrinsically linked. The art of this hymn is evident in how Charles Wesley treated Scripture allegorically: Jacob's spiritual struggle became Wesley's own autobiographical struggle, and, in turn, becomes our story. The hymn is rarely printed in its entirety, often broken into various excerpts. *The United Methodist Hymnal* included both the full original, text-only, and a four-stanza reduction set to music. The final stanza of the reduced form (stanza 9 of the full hymn), in its original wording, bears notice on two points, one of which might be somewhat curious to the modern reader:

> 'Tis love, 'tis love! Thou diedst for me;
>   I hear thy whisper in my heart.
> The morning breaks, the shadows flee:
>   Pure UNIVERSAL LOVE thou art,
> To me, to all thy bowels move,
>   Thy nature, and thy name is love.

If one does a search of "bowels" in the King James Version of the Bible, the version the Wesleys used, it will become apparent how this word appears often throughout Scripture. Citing the *Oxford English Dictionary*, hymnologist J. R. Watson noted how the term "bowels" was quite common in the seventeenth and eighteenth centuries and was "considered as the seat of the tender and sympathetic affections—to mean pity, compassion, feeling, 'heart.'"[3]

The other significant aspect of this stanza is in the way "Wesley's faith journey, as told through his hymn, ends with the revelation that God is 'pure

---

1. Erik Routley, in *Hymns and Human Life* (London: John Murray, 1952) 64, called Watts "the liberator of English hymnody."

2. The hymn was republished in full in *Hymns and Spiritual Songs*, in 24 eds. (1753–1786), with some changes. In *A Collection of Hymns for the Use of the People Called Methodists* (1780), this was reduced to 12 stanzas (1–4, 6, 8–14 of the original).

3. Watson, *Annotated Anthology of Hymns*, 183.

universal love."⁴ "Universal love" is a primary tenet of Wesleyan theology, and it stood in bold contrast to the Calvinist view of the "elect" propagated by their contemporary, George Whitefield (1714–1770), whose powerful preaching drew crowds rivaling those of the Wesleys.

The famous commentary on the Bible by Anglican cleric Matthew Henry (1662–1714) is said to have influenced Wesley's understanding and interpretation of Jacob's dream. Henry set up the scene with a brief overview of chapter 32:

> We have here Jacob still upon his journey towards Canaan. Never did so many memorable things occur in any march, as in this of Jacob's little family. By the way he meets, 1. With good tidings from his God (vs. 1–2); 2. With bad tidings from his brother, to whom he sent a message to notify his return (vs. 2–7). In his distress, 1. He divides his company (vs. 7–8); 2. He makes his prayer to God (vs. 9–12); 3. He sends a present to his brother (vs. 13–23); 4. He wrestles with the angel (vs. 24–32).⁵

Examining closely the complete text of the hymn, it becomes evident how Wesley's version parallels Scripture. The scriptural narrative begins, "And Jacob was left alone; and there wrestled a man with him until the breaking of the day" (Gen 32:24, KJV). The opening stanza cited above concludes with a nearly verbatim quotation from this verse. Henry pointed out how Hosea 12:4 also references this event: "Yea, he had power over the angel, and prevailed: he wept, and made supplication unto him: he found him in Bethel, and there he spake with us" (KJV).

Wesley also drew upon the persistent request found in this passage, "What is thy name?" (Gen 32:27, KJV), "Tell me, I pray thee, thy name" (Gen 32:29). In Wesley's hymn, the question is "Who art thou? Tell me thy name and tell me now." In the complete version, Wesley's insistence continues through several stanzas: "I will not let thee go till thy name, thy nature know." The unknown "NAME" is central to this passage. Henry's commentary noted how there are several interpretations of the "name," but "we are sure God's name was in him," citing Exodus 23:21, "Beware of him, and obey his voice, provoke him not; for he will not pardon your transgressions: for my name is in him" (KJV). At this point, it is clear Wesley was not just writing a scriptural paraphrase, he had merged his own faith struggle into the biblical passage. Wesley's demand

---

4. Young, *Companion*, 295.

5. Matthew Henry, *An Exposition of the Five Books of Moses* (London, 1707), introduction to Genesis 32; also in *An Exposition of All the Books of the Old and New Testament* 1 (1708); available online at https://www.biblestudytools.com/commentaries/matthew-henry-complete/genesis/32.html

to know the name of the one with whom he struggled magnifies that of the biblical narrative several times over through powerful images and repetition.

Keep in mind, during the previous decade before this hymn's publication in 1742, Charles and John had traveled to America, an unsuccessful journey pastorally, professionally, and personally, resulting in a crisis of faith. Only after being offered spiritual guidance by Moravian minister Peter Böhler (1712–1775) did Charles experience his own conversion on Whitsunday (Pentecost), May 21, 1738, following a severe physical illness and perhaps some form of depression. Within a few days, he recorded his conversion in the hymn "Where shall my wondering soul begin":

> Believe, and all your sin's forgiv'n,
> Only believe, and yours is heav'n!

While the first half of the full hymn insists on knowing the nature and name of the Savior, the second half exults in the knowledge of the name when finally revealed: "'Tis Love, 'tis Love! . . . pure UNIVERSAL LOVE . . ." Then the poet repeated six times (!), "Thy Nature, and thy Name is LOVE" (upper case in the original!). This passionate revelation parallels Jacob's (now Israel's) recognition of the one with whom he wrestled: "I have seen God face to face, and my life is preserved" (Gen 32:30, KJV). Carlton Young, *United Methodist Hymnal* editor, noted how the "hymn's central theme is the intense struggle attendant in the changing of one's own heart and being."[6] British hymn scholar J.R. Watson stated, "Wesley is putting himself in the place of Jacob, and encountering God in wrestling with Him as an adversary. As Jacob 'halted upon his thigh' [32:31], so the redeemed sinner is marked by the encounter to the end of his life."[7] The power of this narrative in its original form lies in what Wesley scholar J. Ernest Rattenbury felt was Wesley's ability to tell the story "as if it were an event of his own experience."[8] John Wesley cited this hymn in the obituary tribute to his brother at the Methodist Conference in 1788, noting how Isaac Watts had acknowledged "that single poem, 'Wrestling Jacob,' was worth all the verses he himself had written."[9] Two weeks after Charles Wesley's death, John Wesley, preaching at Bolton on April 19, 1788, attempted to lead this hymn, but struggled:

> [Mr. Haslam was] present in the chapel at Ridgeway Gates when Mr. Wesley visited Bolton, just after Mr. Charles Wesley's death. The venerable man, himself eighty-five years of age, commenced

---

6. Young, *Companion*, 295.
7. Watson, *Annotated Anthology*, 184.
8. Rattenbury, *Evangelical Doctrines*, 96.
9. *Annual Minutes, 1788*, in Baker et al., *Works of John Wesley*, 10:646.

the service in the usual way, with singing and prayer; for the second hymn he selected "Wrestling Jacob" and gave out the first verse with peculiar emphasis. When he came to the words "My company before is gone, and I am left alone with Thee," his emotion became uncontrollable, and he burst right out into a flood of tears, and sat down in the pulpit, covering his face with both hands. The effect upon the congregation was such as might be expected—the people ceased to sing, and, in many parts of the chapel, sat down weeping and sobbing aloud. . . . After awhile, Mr. Wesley recovered himself, arose, and gave out the lines again; "and then there was such singing," said the good old man, "as I never had heard before; it seemed as if the sound would lift the roof of the building."[10]

It is worth one's time to read the entire original fourteen stanzas. Upon reading the poem in its entirety, one cannot help but agree with Anglican hymn writer Timothy Dudley-Smith, who stated in his commentary in the *Canterbury Dictionary of Hymnology*:

> The whole poem is a sustained *tour de force* in which the spontaneous, daring, dramatic emotion and vitality are enhanced by an unobtrusive skill and an astonishing maturity of technique. The 84 lines of the original are remarkable for the urgency and easy flow of the narrative, which yet includes a punctuation mark at the end of almost every line. Similarly the syntax flows with very little inversion. Verses 6, 7, and 8 are also notable for the use of paradox, a feature of much of Charles Wesley's writing, but rarely so effectively displayed as here.[11]

WRESTLING JACOB

> Come, O thou traveller unknown,
>   Whom still I hold, but cannot see!
> My company before is gone,
>   And I am left alone with thee:
> With thee all night I mean to stay,
> And wrestle till the break of day.

---

10. *Homes, Haunts, and Friends*, 21–22, quoting *The Methodist Recorder* of 5 Dec. 1861. See also *Journal and Diaries VII (1787–1791)* in Baker et al., *The Works of John Wesley*, 24:76–77.

11. Timothy Dudley-Smith, "Come, O thou Traveller unknown," in *Canterbury Dictionary of Hymnology*.

I need not tell thee who I am,
    My misery or sin declare;
Thyself hast call'd me by my name;
    Look on thy hands, and read it there!
But who, I ask thee, who art thou?
Tell me thy name, and tell me now.

In vain thou strugglest to get free,
    I never will unloose my hold.
Art thou the man that died for me?
    The secret of thy love unfold;
Wrestling, I will not let thee go,
Till I thy name, thy nature know.

Wilt thou not yet to me reveal
    Thy new, unutterable name?
Tell me, I still[12] beseech thee, tell,
    To know it now, resolv'd I am;
Wrestling I will not let thee go,
Till I thy name, thy nature know.

'Tis all in vain to hold thy tongue,
    Or touch the hollow of my thigh:
Though every sinew were[13] unstrung,
    Out of my arms thou shalt[14] not fly;
Wrestling, I will not let thee go,
Till I thy name, thy nature know.

What though my shrinking flesh complain,
    And murmur to contend so long,
I rise superior to my pain;
    When I am weak, then I am strong;
And when my all of strength shall[15] fail,
I shall with the God-man prevail.

My strength is gone, my nature dies,
    I sink beneath thy weighty hand,
Faint to revive, and fall to rise;
    I fall, and yet by faith I stand;

12. O tell me, I : *HSS*, eds. 5–24 (1758–1786).
13. be : *HSP* (1742).
14. shouldst : *HSS*, eds. 1–8 (1753–1761).
15. doth : *HSS*, all eds. (1753–1786).

I stand, and will not let thee go,
Till I thy name, thy nature know.

Yield to me now—for I am weak,
    But confident in self-despair!
Speak to my heart, in blessings speak,
    Be conquer'd by my instant prayer;
Speak, or thou never hence shalt[16] move,
And tell me, if thy name is love.

'Tis love! 'tis love! thou diedst for me!
    I hear thy whisper in my heart.
The morning breaks, the shadows flee:
    Pure UNIVERSAL LOVE thou art,
To me, to all thy bowels move,
Thy nature, and thy name is love.

My prayer hath power with God; the grace
    Unspeakable I now receive,
Through faith I see thee face to face;
    I see thee face to face, and live!
In vain I have not wept and[17] strove;
Thy nature, and thy name is love.

I know thee, Saviour, who thou art,
    Jesus, the feeble sinner's friend;
Nor wilt thou with the night depart,
    But stay, and love me to the end;
Thy mercies never shall remove,
Thy nature, and thy name is love.

The Sun of Righteousness on me
    Hath rose, with healing in his wings;
Wither'd my nature's strength; from thee
    My soul its life and succour brings;
My help is all laid up above;
Thy nature, and thy name is love.

Contented now, upon my thigh
    I halt, till life's short journey end;
All helplesness, all weakness I,

---

16. shall : *HSS*, eds. 7-15 (1759-1771), 18-24 (1774-1786).
17. nor : *HSS*, 19th ed. (1775); or : *HSS*, eds. 20-24 (1776-1786).

On thee alone for strength depend,
Nor have I power from thee to move;
Thy nature, and thy name is love.

Lame as I am, I take the prey,
    Hell, earth, and sin with ease o'ercome;
I leap for joy, pursue my way,
    And as a bounding hart fly home,
Through all eternity to prove
Thy nature, and thy name is love.[18]

---

18. A version of this article previously appeared online in Hawn, *History of Hymns*.

Incarnation & Resurrection

6

Come, Thou long-expected Jesus

JOSH DEAR

While Charles Wesley is known today almost exclusively by his hymns, he actually had a much broader ministry, which included, among other things, a great deal of preaching. As Stephen J. Nichols explained, "Charles Wesley was an effective preacher in his own right. His sermons, when published, outsold his brother's."[1] T. Crichton Mitchell regarded Charles as "one of the most formative figures in the history of the modern church," and while he obviously lived under the shadow of his brother John, "had he been half as diligent as John in keeping a journal, preserving his letters, and exposing his personal and domestic life, the shadow would not have been so heavy."[2] Nevertheless, his most enduring contribution to the church has surely been the theologically rich hymns God enabled him to write. History reveals to us how "Methodism was born in song,"[3] and Charles Wesley was largely responsible for that, as he wrote so many of the songs Christians around the world—especially Methodists—have loved to sing for generations.

Much like his brother John, Charles loved God's Word. His growing knowledge of Scripture not only served as sufficient food for his own soul, but also contributed to the rich and edifying content of his sermons, poems, and numerous hymns. According to one biographer, "Charles after his conversion became a 'man of one book' and so saturated with the Bible that

1. Nichols, *Pages from Church History*, 267.
2. Mitchell, *Charles Wesley*, 11.
3. Langford, "Charles Wesley as Theologian," 97.

if much of Holy Writ were to be destroyed, it could with no great labour be pieced together from the mosaic of his hymns."[4] Wesley's Advent hymn "Come, Thou long-expected Jesus" serves as one example of the theological poetry born out of his fruitful engagement with the Word of God.

"Come, Thou long-expected Jesus" was first published on December 17, 1745[5]—the day before Charles Wesley's 38th birthday—as part of a small collection, *Hymns for the Nativity of Our Lord*. The hymnal contained only eighteen Christmas hymns, published without music, titles, or headings (this was the tenth hymn in the collection). This small booklet was published in twenty-seven editions through 1791.[6]

Charles Wesley was known for having "a theology one can sing,"[7] meaning he had an obvious gifting from God for expressing the profound doctrines of Scripture in memorable, poetic verse. In *Hymns for the Nativity of Our Lord*, the theological focus of Wesley's lyrics was the vital role of the Incarnation in God's eternal plan of salvation. As J. Ernest Rattenbury observed, "It is perhaps significant that there is hardly mention of the Cross in the Nativity hymns, but that the object of the Incarnation was the salvation of the world is declared repeatedly. Reconciliation, [atonement], begins with the Incarnation."[8] He further noted, "from the manger to the cross Charles Wesley saw in Christ God manifest in the flesh and realized never more than at the manger that the flesh with which God clad himself was very human."[9] In his nativity hymns, Wesley aimed to provoke awe and wonder by drawing our attention to the ultimate act of condescension: God becoming man in the Incarnation of Jesus for the sake of lost sinners, who—without God's divine intervention—would remain lost and separated from God for eternity.

Regarding *Hymns for the Nativity of Our Lord*, T. Crichton Mitchell explained, "By near unanimous opinion, this pamphlet is among Wesley's best. Whereas in the Trinitarian pamphlet he accentuates in such a manner as to leave no doubt about his faith in the divinity of the Lord Jesus Christ, in this pamphlet the accentuation expresses his belief in the real and true humanity of the Lord Jesus Christ."[10] Furthermore, he said the lyrics "are

---

4. Brailsford, *A Tale of Two Brothers*, 138.

5. For the publication date, often erroneously reported as 1744, see especially *Nativity Hymns* in Maddox, *Charles Wesley's Published Verse*.

6. Maddox, *Nativity Hymns*, ii.

7. Langford, "Charles Wesley as Theologian," 97.

8. Rattenbury, *Evangelical Doctrines*, 169.

9. Rattenbury, *Evangelical Doctrines*, 172.

10. Mitchell, *Charles Wesley*, 196. The "Trinitarian pamphlet" is *Gloria Patri; or Hymns to the Trinity* (1746).

sprinkled with vivid, arresting, and provocative phrases as well as soul-lifting and exhilarating thought. The spirit is that of adoration and wonder."[11] This conviction is shared by other scholars as well, such as Randy Maddox, who wrote, "This collection contains some of Wesley's most creative work . . . [and] some of his most compelling images about the paradoxical affirmation of the Divine becoming human."[12]

In spite of the apparent popularity of Wesley's nativity hymns when they were first published, most of the songs in *Hymns for the Nativity of Our Lord* have not retained their popularity in our own day. In fact, "Come, Thou long-expected Jesus" seems to be the only hymn in the collection to have endured, becoming Charles Wesley's second-most popular Christmas hymn next to "Hark! the herald angels sing." As a testament to the hymn's quality, timelessness, and ability to reach across denominational and theological differences, it quickly found its way into the collections of both friends and critics of the Wesleys, including Martin Madan's *Collection of Psalms and Hymns* (1760) and Augustus Toplady's *Psalms and Hymns for Public and Private Worship* (1776).

Consider especially Charles's contemporary George Whitefield (1714–1770), an Anglican minister who helped found the Methodist movement, even though—unlike John and Charles Wesley—he was a Calvinist. The theological disputes between Whitefield and John Wesley regarding God's sovereignty, predestination, and the doctrine of election strained their relationship greatly, though they continued to hold one another in high regard and maintained a mutual appreciation for each other's devotion to God. When a fellow Calvinist once approached George Whitefield to ask if he believed they would see John Wesley in heaven, Whitefield is said to have replied, "I do not think we shall. . . . I am afraid that you and I will be so far off the throne of Christ, and Wesley will be so near, that he will be lost in the brightness of his Saviour, and I hardly think you and I will be able to see him."[13]

The Wesleys grew to share a similar respect for Whitefield's ministry, even warning their preachers near the end of the 1740s to resist the urge to speak publicly against Calvinistic teaching, especially regarding the doctrine of predestination. Charles Wesley once wrote, "G.W., and my brother and I, are one, a threefold cord, which shall no more be broken," and went

---

11. T. Crichton Mitchell, *Charles Wesley*, 196.
12. Randy L. Maddox, *Nativity Hymns*, i.
13. Spurgeon, *The Two Wesleys*, 6.

on to express his genuine appreciation for George and his sincere regrets for their past dissension.[14] He expressed this in a poem as well:

> Come on, my Whitefield! (since the strife is past,
> And friends at first are friends again at last)
> Our hands, and hearts, and counsels let us join
> In mutual league, t'advance the work Divine,
> Our concentration now, our single aim,
> To pluck poor souls as brands out of the flame;
> To spread the victory of that bloody cross,
> And gasp our latest breath in the Redeemer's cause.[15]

John Wesley penned similar thoughts about Whitefield in his diary, writing on November 5, 1755: "Disputings are now no more. We love one another and join hand in hand to promote the cause of our common Master."[16] As history shows, this mutual friendship between Whitefield and the Wesley brothers continued for the rest of their lives, to the very day when John Wesley—in response to Whitefield's earlier request—preached at the funeral of George Whitefield, November 18, 1770, at which John said, "Most appeared to be deeply affected."[17] A few weeks later, on January 2, 1771, he wrote, "In every place, I wish to show all possible respect to the memory of that great and good man."[18]

Whitefield's appreciation for the Wesleys proved far greater than his criticism of their doctrinal views. This became evident as he made use of Charles Wesley's hymns in public worship. He published a number of the Wesleys' hymns in *A Collection of Hymns for Social Worship* (1753), and "Come, Thou long-expected Jesus" was among them.[19] The intentional effort between these brothers of divergent theological persuasions to be reconciled to one another not only served as a beautiful model of Christian unity and love, but it also helped to increase the popularity of Charles Wesley's hymns.

Another famous preacher whose theological differences did not hinder him from making use of Wesley's hymns was Charles Haddon Spurgeon

---

14. Letter to Ebenezer Blackwell, 8 October 1749, in Jackson, *Journal of Charles Wesley, M.A.*, 2:178.

15. *An Epistle to the Reverend Mr George Whitefield* (1771).

16. Baker et al., *Works of John Wesley*, 21:33.

17. Baker et al., *Works of John Wesley*, 22:259.

18. Baker et al., *Works of John Wesley*, 22:261.

19. "Come, Thou long-expected Jesus" was not included in the first edition (1753), but it appeared in the first supplement, with the 5th ed. (1756), then in every subsequent edition. See also Justin Taylor, "George Whitefield's Gospel-Centered Hymn Book," in *The Gospel Coalition*.

(1834–1892). In a sermon he preached on December 23, 1855, "The Incarnation and Birth of Christ," Spurgeon made reference to this hymn and acknowledged it to be a hymn he and his congregation at New Park Street Chapel had already been singing as part of their Christmas-time worship (though Spurgeon regarded Christmas as being no more special a day than any other time of year for proclaiming the joyful message of the Incarnation of Christ). In this sermon, Spurgeon made the following point:

> I remember no one who was born a king except Jesus; and there is emphatic meaning in that verse that we sing—"Born thy people to deliver; Born a child, and yet a king." The moment that he came on earth he was a king. He did not wait till his majority that he might take his empire; but as soon as his eye greeted the sunshine he was a king; from the moment that his little hands grasped anything, they grasped a sceptre; as soon as his pulse beat, and his blood began to flow, his heart beat royally, and his pulse an imperial measure, and his blood flowed in a kingly current. He was born a king.[20]

Although Charles Spurgeon, being an avowed Calvinist, had some significant theological differences with both John and Charles Wesley, his respect and appreciation for the Wesley brothers only seemed to grow over time. On December 6, 1861, Spurgeon gave an inspiring public lecture titled "The Two Wesleys," in which he declared, "It will be time for us to find fault with John and Charles Wesley, not when we discover their mistakes, but when we have cured our own. When we shall have more piety than they, more fire, more grace, more burning love, more intense unselfishness, then, and not till then, may we begin to find fault and criticize."[21] Like Whitefield, Spurgeon included "Come, Thou long-expected Jesus" in his congregational hymnal, *Our Own Hymn-Book* (1866). Spurgeon's gracious acknowledgement of the Wesleys' fruitful ministry and his endorsement of some of Charles Wesley's hymns for use within his own church illustrates just how far-reaching was the acceptance and influence of Charles Wesley's hymns, even beyond some of the denominational lines which might otherwise divide believers in their worship of God.

---

20. Spurgeon, "The Incarnation and Birth of Christ," 2:29.
21. Spurgeon, *The Two Wesleys*, 63.

TEXTUAL ANALYSIS

"Come, Thou long-expected Jesus" seems to have a multi-layered purpose: first, to remind us of the eager anticipation the ancient Israelites had for the promised Messiah's arrival on earth, and second, to express the even greater anticipation God's people have today for the final return of Jesus, who is the ultimate culmination and fulfillment of all the promises of God given to us in the New Testament. Hymnologist Carl Daw Jr. expressed this well in his brief summary of the hymn:

> Despite the title of the collection in which this text was published, and despite the four appearances of "born" here, this is not so much a hymn about Nativity as it is about Incarnation. The details of the birth are never mentioned: no manger, no shepherds, no angels. Yet there is an awareness here that the larger mystery being celebrated leads to the sending of the Holy Spirit and comes full circle in Christ's reign in glory, when God's people will find freedom from fear and sin, when hope will be fulfilled, and when human hearts will be aligned with God's saving purposes."[22]

C. Michael Hawn has recognized in these lyrics a sense of petition, or a prayer imploring Christ to come and dwell among us, noting Wesley's use of imperative verbs: "Come," "release," "let," "bring," "rule," "raise." "The cumulative effect," he observed, "is a tone of supplication," as the one praying (or, in this case, singing) entreats the Lord to come and bring peace and freedom for all his people, just as they've been expecting him to do for some time. By zealously petitioning the Lord in this way, Hawn said, "Wesley succeeds in recalling the deep longing of ancient Israel for the Messiah—the Promised One."[23]

Hawn also observed how the repetition of the word "born"—while not actually intended to describe the circumstances of the divine birth—offers four particular reasons for the Incarnation of Christ. Why exactly did Jesus come, according to these lyrics from Wesley? He was born (1) to set his people free, (2) to deliver his people, (3) to be our king, and (4) to reign in us forever.[24] How edifying it is for God's people to consider the ways in which Christ, through both the Incarnation and his Second Coming, fulfills each of these purposes in God's eternal plan of redemption!

---

22. Daw, "Come, thou long-expected Jesus," 82–84.
23. Hawn, "Hymn expresses longing," in *History of Hymns*.
24. Hawn, "Hymn expresses longing," in *History of Hymns*.

Wesley scholar S.T. Kimbrough, in noting the hymn's references to freedom ("Born to set thy people free," "From our fears and sins release us," "Born thy people to deliver"), perceived a strong influence in Wesley's first-hand exposure to human slavery.[25] After spending five discouraging months in the American colony of Georgia, Charles retreated to England. While passing through Charleston, he witnessed violent demonstrations of the abuse of slaves, which affected him very deeply. In his journal for August 2, 1736, he noted:

> I had observed much, and heard more, of the cruelty of masters towards their negroes. But now I received an authentic account of some horrid instances thereof. The giving a child a slave of its own age to tyrannize over, to beat and abuse out of sport, was, I myself saw, a common practice. Nor is it strange that being thus trained up in cruelty, they should afterwards arrive at so great perfection in it; that Mr. Star, a gentleman I often met at Mr. Laserre's should, as he himself informed Laserre, first nail up a negro by the ears, then order him to be whipped in the severest manner, and then to have scalding water thrown all over him, so that the poor creature could not stir for four months after.... These horrid cruelties are the less to be wondered at, because the government itself, in effect, countenances and allows them to kill their slaves by the ridiculous penalty appointed for it, of about seven pounds sterling (half of which is usually saved by the criminal's informing against himself). This I can look upon as no other than a public act to indemnify murder."[26]

Notice how his rebuke of the government for this atrocity is reflected in his hymn's allusion to Haggai 2:7, "And I will shake all nations, and the desire of all nations shall come: and I will fill this house with glory saith the Lord of hosts" (KJV). This passage is often understood to be a foretelling of the coming of Christ, since Jesus would be the ultimate "desire of all nations," whose coming truly would "shake all nations." The hopeful promise of Haggai's prophecy serves as a striking contrast to the wickedness of slavery, and this distinction might have been used by God to provoke the heart and mind of Charles Wesley as he wrote these lyrics proclaiming the freedom found in Christ alone.

---

25. Kimbrough, *A Heart to Praise My God*, 84–85.
26. Kimbrough and Newport, *Manuscript Journal*, 1:46–47.

STANZA 1

> Come, thou long-expected Jesus,
>   Born to set thy people free;
> From our fears and sins release[27] us;
>   Let us find our rest in thee.
> Israel's strength and consolation,
>   Hope of all the earth thou art;
> Dear desire of ev'ry nation,
>   Joy of ev'ry longing heart.

From the first line of the hymn, the allusions to Scripture are numerous and clear. In the Old Testament, there is an obvious theme of expectation regarding the promised Messiah who would someday come and redeem God's people, with specific prophecies concerning his virgin birth (Isa 7:14), the location of his birth (Mic 5:2), the glorious ways in which he would change the world (Isa 9:6–7), the suffering he would endure for our sake and the atonement for sin he would accomplish by his death and resurrection (Isa 53). However, as J. Ligon Duncan acknowledged, the saints of old did not know the name "Jesus" and didn't have the privilege of calling him by name as we do today. He explained, "We sing the name of the Messiah back to God, whereas the old covenant saint could only look forward to His coming."[28] This, in itself, suggests how the hymn is not merely intended for us as a remembrance of what the earliest believers prayed while they anticipated the arrival of the Lord, but it is also intended for our own sincere worship of Christ as we look ahead to his imminent return (Rev 22:20).

Line two declares one of the reasons why Jesus took on human flesh, which was to set people free (Isa 61:1; Luke 4:18; Rom 8:2), while line three clarifies what Jesus came to deliver his people from: the guilt and consequences of sin, and the fear of condemnation. In Christ, we may receive forgiveness for our sins, reconciliation with God, and full pardon from God's terrible and eternal judgment (1 Tim 1:15). In line four, Wesley's lyrics remind us to be sure our hope and trust are in Jesus alone, since he alone is able to save us, and they offer us a joyful reminder that in him, we will ultimately find rest because of the divine peace given to all who truly belong to God (Ps 29:11; Matt 11:29).

Lines five through eight joyfully proclaim some of the ways Jesus satisfies the deepest longings of God's people. For the ancient Israelites, Jesus would become their "strength and consolation," strengthening and

---

27. relieve : *Nativity Hymns*, eds. 1745–1774.

28. J. Ligon Duncan, "Come, Thou Long Expected Jesus," in *First Presbyterian Church* (Jackson, MS).

comforting all who came to him with heavy burdens and hurting hearts (1 Sam 15:29; Pss 46:1–3; 68:35; 2 Cor 12:9). And we know he does the same for his people today! The next lines remind us how Jesus didn't come only for Israel, but for all nations of the world.

The deepest longing and greatest need of every person is true and lasting salvation, and Wesley's lyrics make it clear, Jesus alone is able to meet this need (John 14:6). God's incomparable gift of salvation, which is able to meet the greatest needs of sinful humanity, is offered here in a particular order: first, globally ("to all the earth"), then, to individual nations ("ev'ry nation"), and finally, to individual people ("ev'ry longing heart").[29] Both individually and corporately—locally and around the world—true salvation may only be found through our Lord, Jesus Christ, who died on the cross and rose from the grave to atone for the sins of his people.

STANZA 2

> Born thy people to deliver,
>   Born a child and yet a king.
> Born to reign in us forever,
>   Now thy gracious kingdom bring.
> By thine[30] own eternal Spirit
>   Rule in all our hearts alone;
> By thine[31] all-sufficient merit,
>   Raise us to thy glorious throne.

The second stanza begins by giving us three more reasons for the Incarnation of Jesus. First, he came to deliver his people (Matt 1:21). This, of course, sounds very similar to the purpose given in the first stanza, "to set thy people free." Nonetheless, we can perhaps see a distinction in the way the image portrayed by the first expression is of God's people being released from their bondage, whereas the expression here—"to deliver"—might be understood as not only delivering God's people *away from* something, such as their sinful pasts, but also delivering them *to* something, such as an eternally restored relationship with their loving heavenly Father (John 5:24; 1 Pet 2:9–10). How encouraging it is to consider how one of the reasons why

---

29. While the summary of the Great Commission as it is recorded in Acts 1:8 calls for us to proclaim the gospel locally first then move increasingly outward, Wesley's hymn uses the opposite pattern: beginning globally and then working down to the individual, to indicate the sufficiency of the gospel of Jesus Christ to meet the deepest needs of all who will come to him.

30. thy : *Nativity Hymns*, eds. 1762–1791.

31. thy : *Nativity Hymns*, eds. 1762–1791.

Jesus came to earth was to atone for our sins on the cross, purchasing us with his own blood, in order to present us to the heavenly Father, blameless and pure, to live with God for eternity!

Second, Jesus came to assume his rightful place as king. The kingship of Jesus is an obvious theme in the Bible (Mark 13:26; Rev 17:14; 19:16), but it is also one of the great ironies of Scripture—the one who is born as a child, in the most humble and unlikely circumstances, was actually the King of all kings whose rule will never end (1 Tim 6:15; Rev 1:5; 17:14).

Third, Wesley's lyrics remind us how Jesus came "to reign in us forever." He came not only to rule in the world, but also to rule in the hearts of his people (Luke 1:33; Rev 1:6). The full display of God's all-powerful rule is not something to be feared among those of us who love Jesus, but it is something to be desired and greatly anticipated. This is why the fourth line of this second stanza petitions God to bring his gracious kingdom to us *now*. We should all be eager for God's rule over our lives to increase, and for our own self-centered rule over our lives to decrease. The biblical prayers remind us to think this way, as we learn from David to pray, "Search me, O God, and know my heart" (Ps 139:23), and as we learn from Jesus to pray, "Thy kingdom come, Thy will be done" (Matt 6:10). It shouldn't be our own desires which we seek to live out each day, but God's. As we increasingly invite Jesus to rule in our daily lives and seek to do what pleases him, he will be more greatly honored and we will be more greatly blessed.

Lines five and six petition God to be the only Lord of our lives, casting out any selfish desires or secret sins which might still be lingering in our hearts and minds. These lines remind us how it is only through the power and authority of God's Spirit that this transforming work may be accomplished within us (Ezek 36:27). We can't do this in our own abilities; we are desperately dependent upon God to do this important work for us. Significantly, this song doesn't just prompt us to ask God to do this for ourselves, but also for our neighbors, as we join together in singing for God to rule in "all our hearts."

The last two lines of Wesley's hymn petition God to save us fully from our sins, and to bring us into everlasting communion with God, based purely on the merits of Jesus Christ. Apart from the atoning work of Jesus on the cross, we would all remain eternally lost and would face God's wrath as the just punishment for our sins (Rom 3:23; 6:23), but praise be to God, we are not without hope! Though our own works can only condemn us before God (Isa 64:6–7), the work of Christ—his death, burial, and resurrection—is completely sufficient to atone for the sins of all who turn to him in faith. There is obviously some anticipation of our future glorification intended by the phrase "Raise us to thy glorious throne," but this could also be understood in a more immediate sense, as we desire for God to not only bring us into his eternal presence when die, but also to draw us ever-nearer to himself during our earthly lives, as we work to know God more deeply and to obey him more faithfully every day.

ADDENDUM

As it was written by Charles Wesley in 1745, "Come, Thou long-expected Jesus" consisted of only the two stanzas discussed above. However, a more recent hymn writer, Mark E. Hunt, wrote two additional stanzas, which are sometimes inserted as the middle verses of the hymn. These two new stanzas were written for *Carols*,[32] a collection Hunt co-edited for InterVarsity Press, and have been included in other hymn collections.

> Joy to those who long to see thee,
>   Dayspring from on high, appear;
> Come, thou promised Rod of Jesse,
>   Of thy birth we long to hear!
> O'er the hills the angels singing
>   News, glad tidings of a birth:
> "Go to him, your praises bringing;
>   Christ the Lord has come to earth."
>
> Come to earth to taste our sadness,
>   He whose glories knew no end;
> By his life he brings us gladness,
>   Our Redeemer, Shepherd, Friend.
> Leaving riches without number,
>   Born within a cattle stall;
> This the everlasting wonder,
>   Christ was born the Lord of all.

These new stanzas serve as a fitting complement to Wesley's original lyrics in that while Wesley stressed the eternal significance of the Incarnation in his two stanzas, Hunt's lyrics recall the immediate joy and exuberant rejoicing, on earth as well as in heaven, which accompanied the Savior's birth. For hundreds of years, God had promised to send a Messiah who would redeem his people from their sins and secure their salvation forever. The birth of Jesus served as the long-anticipated fulfillment of those glorious promises from God. As angels appeared to Mary, Joseph, and the shepherds proclaiming "good tidings of great joy" (Luke 2:10), God was answering the

---

32. Hunt and Huffman, *Carols*, 63.

deepest longings of their hearts and revealing his eternal plan for their—and our—redemption. While Wesley's lyrics proclaim the glory and goodness of Jesus, reminding us to find our greatest joy in him and to eagerly anticipate his return, Hunt's lyrics reflect back upon the miraculous birth of Jesus, rejoicing in Jesus as our incomparable gift and expressing our deepest gratitude for his coming to earth to redeem us from our sins.

CONCLUSION

This beautiful Advent hymn, though short, is a profound reminder of how the very same Messiah—who once took on flesh, dwelt among us, and called the lost to repent of their sins and proclaim the Good News of God's salvation—will soon return in power and glory. Just as the people of ancient Israel longed for their Savior to come and deliver them from bondage, so should we, with increasing excitement, long for Jesus to return again for his people, to set all things right, and to bring about the final culmination of all God has promised to us in the pages of Scripture. With Charles Wesley, and with a multitude of saints around the world, we look ahead to the final return of Christ and to the sweet fellowship we so eagerly anticipate in the new heavens and the new earth.[33]

---

33. This chapter is lovingly dedicated to three amazing ladies: my mother, Gloria, who raised me to love Jesus and to honor him with my life; to my beautiful wife, Karen, who loves the great hymns and lives out their glorious truths daily; and to Donna Rademacher, a dear friend of our family, who first taught me to sing God's praises (as my childhood choir director) and now continues to inspire many through her abiding love for the hymns of Charles Wesley. I thank God for each of you, and pray for the love and joy evident in your lives to become increasingly evident in my own life, too!

7

Hark! the herald angels sing

CHRIS FENNER

The Wesleys had a lifelong connection and friendship with George Whitefield (1714–1770), beginning with their Oxford Holy Club, followed by separate missionary journeys to America, and a call to open-air field preaching in England. During the earlier years of that association, the Wesleys published some of their most enduring poetry, especially in the first edition of *Hymns and Sacred Poems* (1739). In this collection, Charles Wesley had penned a Christmas hymn with a curious opening line:

> Hark how all the welkin rings,
> "Glory to the King of Kings,
> Peace on Earth, and mercy mild,
> God and sinners reconcil'd!"
>
> Joyful all ye nations rise,
> Join the triumph of the skies,
> Universal nature say,
> "Christ the Lord is born today!"
>
> Christ, by highest Heav'n ador'd,
> Christ, the everlasting Lord,
> Late in time behold him come,
> Offspring of a virgin's womb.

Veil'd in flesh, the Godhead see,
Hail th'incarnate Deity!
Pleas'd as man with men t'appear,
Jesus, our Immanuel here!

Hail the heav'nly Prince of Peace!
Hail the Sun of Righteousness!
Light and life to all he brings,
Ris'n with healing in his wings.

Mild he lays his glory by,
Born—that man no more may die,
Born—to raise the sons of earth,
Born—to give them second birth.

Come, Desire of Nations, come,
Fix in us thy humble home,
Rise, the woman's conqu'ring seed,
Bruise in us the serpent's head.

Now display thy saving pow'r,
Ruin'd nature now restore,
Now in mystic union join
Thine to ours, and ours to thine.

Adam's likeness, Lord, efface,
Stamp thy image in its place,
Second Adam from above,
Reinstate us in thy love.

Let us thee, tho' lost, regain,
Thee, the life, the inner man;
O! to all thyself impart,
Form'd in each believing heart.

Wesley's original text thus spanned ten stanzas of four lines. A modern reader might see the words "welkin rings" and immediately gravitate to something from J.R.R. Tolkien, but "welkin" means "sky" or "heavens"—it was a common term in English poetry in that era. In this line, Wesley might have been alluding to a poem by William Somerville about fox hunting, called "The Chase" (1735):

> The welkin rings, Men, Dogs, Hills, Rock, and Woods
> In the full consort join.

Hymn scholar J.R. Watson explained:

> To have altered Somerville's lines would have been in keeping with Wesley's habit of appropriating images from other poems and using them to proclaim the gospel. Here the cries of the huntsmen and hounds become the sounds of the multitude of the heavenly host, praising God, and saying, "Glory to God in the highest."[1]

In the second edition of *Hymns and Sacred Poems* (1739), Wesley made one minor change to the first line of the fifth stanza, which became "Hail the heaven-born Prince of Peace."

As clever as Wesley's allusion to welkin rings might have been, it failed to resonate with some worshipers, including his colleague George Whitefield. In 1753, the same year Whitefield began construction on the Tabernacle church, he compiled his own hymnal, *A Collection of Hymns for Social Worship*. It contained 21 hymns from the Wesleys, including this Christmas hymn, but with a significant alteration:

> Hark! the Herald Angels sing
> Glory to the new-born King!

Whitefield made other alterations as well, including the second stanza, lines 3–4, "Nature rise and worship Him, who is born at Bethlehem," the fifth stanza, "Light and life *around* he brings," the seventh stanza, "Fix in us thy *heav'nly* home," the omission of stanzas eight and ten, and a change in the last line of stanza nine, "*Work it in us* by thy love."

Whitefield was not the only one who felt compelled to tweak Wesley's text. Another close colleague of the Wesleys, Martin Madan (1725–1790), had an important hand in shaping the text. Madan had been called into a life of ministry via the preaching of John Wesley, and he was godfather to Charles Wesley's son Samuel. In 1760, he published *A Collection of Psalms and Hymns*, including Wesley's Christmas hymn. Madan borrowed Whitefield's opening lines but kept the rest of Wesley's original wording, except in the second stanza, where he introduced the lines "With th' angelic host proclaim, Christ is born in Bethlehem!"

John Wesley chose not to include this hymn in the career-spanning *Collection of Hymns for the Use of the People Called Methodists* (1780). A few years later, after being entreated to produce a smaller, more affordable collection, he published *A Pocket Hymn Book*, first in 1785, then greatly revised in 1787. For the revised edition, he added the Christmas hymn, but he decided to use Madan's version, which by extension also included

---

1. Watson, "Welkins," 80.

Whitefield's opening lines. Therefore, the last official Wesleyan version of the hymn looked like this:

> Hark! the herald angels sing,
> "Glory to their new-born King;
> Peace on earth, and mercy mild;
> God and sinners reconciled."
> Joyful, all ye nations, rise,
> Join the triumph of the skies,
> With th' angelic host proclaim,
> "Christ is born in Bethlehem."
>
> Christ, by highest heaven adored,
> Christ, the everlasting Lord;
> Late in time behold him come,
> Offspring of a virgin's womb;
> Veiled in flesh, the Godhead see,
> Hail th' incarnate Deity!
> Pleased as man with men to appear,
> Jesus our Immanuel here.
>
> Hail, the heaven-born Prince of Peace,
> Hail, the Sun of Righteousness!
> Light and life to all he brings,
> Risen with healing in his wongs;
> Mild he lays his glory by,
> Born that man no more may die,
> Born to raise the sons of earth,
> Born to give them second birth.
>
> Come, desire of nations, come,
> Fix in us thy humble home;
> Rise, the woman's conquering seed;
> Bruise in us the serpent's head:
> Adam's likeness now efface,
> Stamp thine image in its place;
> Second Adam from above,
> Reinstate us in thy love.

The first stanza of the hymn is essentially a retelling of the story of the angels and the shepherds in Luke 2. The second stanza introduces several ideas. Christ is worshiped by the hosts of heaven, which is seen especially in the book of Revelation. Christ is everlasting, or eternal, an idea expressed in Hebrews 13:8 ("Jesus Christ is the same yesterday and today and forever,"

ESV). The phrase "late in time" probably refers to the lengthy wait the Jews endured while anticipating their Messiah, and the long absence of any prophet in Israel. The virgin, of course, is Mary, the woman prophesied in Isaiah 7:14. The concept of God-made-flesh can be found in passages such as John 1:14 ("And the Word became flesh and dwelt among us"). Jesus was not too proud to be seen in human form among sinful people, as in Philippians 2:5–7.

In the third stanza, the name "Prince of Peace" comes from Isaiah 9:6. Both the title "Sun of Righteousness" and the image "Risen with healing in his wings" come from Malachi 4:2. The emphatic repetition of "Born . . ." outlines three reasons for Christ's presence: (1) to conquer death, (2) to bring resurrection of the dead, and (3) to offer rebirth, the first two of which are described at length in 1 Corinthians 15, the last best expressed in John 3.

Another title, "Desire of nations," is from Haggai 2:7 (especially in the KJV). The notion of Christ dwelling *in* us, not just *with* us, is reflected in passages like Galatians 2:20 ("I have been crucified with Christ. It is no longer I who live, but Christ who lives in me"). The last six lines point back to Eden in various ways. "Rise, the woman's conquering seed," etc., refers to the Eden prophecy of Genesis 3:15. The remaining lines about exchanging the image of Adam for the image of Christ, with Christ as the "second Adam," reflect the ideas found in 1 Corinthians 15:45–49.

The hymn in this form, written by Charles Wesley, altered by George Whitefield, altered again by Martin Madan, then canonized by John Wesley, is therefore rich with Scripture. Its endurance as a beloved Christmas tradition is well deserved and is likely to last for generations to come.[2]

---

2. Versions of this article have previously appeared in *Towers*, The Southern Baptist Theological Seminary, 13/4 (Nov. 2014) 20, and online at HymnologyArchive.com.

8

Christ the Lord is ris'n today

JOE HARROD

Appearing under the heading of "Hymn for Easter-Day" in *Hymns and Sacred Poems* (1739), this hymn is a tremendous text commemorating Christ's resurrection.[1] As Wesley scholar Randy Maddox has noted, *Hymns and Sacred Poems* contained Charles Wesley's earliest published verse and was the first distinctively Methodist hymnal.[2] The Wesleys released the hymnal in March of 1739, approximately ten months after Charles Wesley's evangelical conversion (May 21, 1738). In his journal, John noted Easter was celebrated on April 22 that year; it is possible this hymn was first sung publicly on that date among the Wesleys and their supporters.[3] In the 1739 collection, this hymn was part of a cycle of hymns marking the church year,

---

1. *Hymns and Sacred Poems* [HSP] (1739), revised in the 4th ed. (1743), and included in the Dublin ed. (1747). The first stanza appeared with music in *A Collection of Tunes . . . Sung at the Foundery* (1742) and in *Sacred Harmony* (1780). A manuscript copy ca. 1746 survives in MS Richmond Tracts (MA 1977/423), John Rylands Library, The University of Manchester.

2. Maddox, *Hymns and Sacred Poems* (1739), in *Charles Wesley's Published Verse*.

3. Unfortunately, the brothers recorded little about their services that day. John's journal said, "On Easter Day, it being a thorough rain, I could only preach at Newgate at eight in the morning and two in the afternoon, in a house near Hanham Mount at eleven, and in one near Rose Green at five. At the society in the evening many were cut to the heart and many comforted," in Baker et al., *Works of John Wesley*, 19:50. Charles said, "Talked with the Count [Zinzendorf] about motions, visions, dreams, and was confirmed in my dislike to them," in Kimbrough and Newport, *Manuscript Journal*, 1:171.

including the Christmas hymn "Hark how all the welkin rings" ("Hark, the herald angels sing").

The first line of Wesley's resurrection text imitates the earlier English hymn "Jesus Christ is risen today" from *Lyra Davidica* (1708), itself an anonymous paraphrase of fourteenth-century Latin hymn *Surrexit Christus hodie*.[4] Like the Latin text, Wesley's hymn features rhyming couplets, yet Wesley's meter is trochaic rather than iambic.[5] The original hymn has eleven stanzas, but most hymnals retain only around half of them.[6] The familiar "alleluia" refrain was not written in Charles's text, but it is added when singing the SALISBURY tune, as reflected in the Wesleys' *Collection of Tunes . . . Sung at the Foundery* (1742). The following analysis notes the biblical allusions and theological convictions woven throughout the stanzas of the hymn and emphasizes key elements of its spirituality.

STANZA 1

> "Christ the Lord is ris'n to day,"
> Sons of men and angels say;
> Raise your joys and triumphs high;
> Sing ye heav'ns, and earth reply.

Wesley began his hymn with a paraphrase of the angelic announcement in Mark 16:6, "He is risen; he is not here" (KJV).[7] Joining with the angel, the "Sons of men" are either Christ's disciples who found his tomb empty, or the countless generations of Christians who continue to celebrate this event. Lines two and four make a chiasm: human witnesses echo the angelic pronouncement, and the message of both is one of celebration and victory.

> Sons of men and angels say . . .
> Sing ye heav'ns, and earth reply.

---

4. "The Resurrection," in *Lyra Davidica* (London: J. Walsh, 1708). For a helpful discussion of the Latin text and its various translations and adaptations, see Fenner, "Surrexit Christus hodie." The Latin hymn has been adapted for contemporary usage by the Taizé Community Choir in *Songs of Taizé* (Integrity Music, 1999).

5. See Fenner, "Surrexit Christus hodie" for this analysis and for more on the background of the Latin. Wesley's stanzas feature four lines with seven syllables whereas the Latin stanzas are eight syllables in two lines.

6. To give a few examples within Methodism: Madan, *Collection of Psalms and Hymns* (1760), uses sts. 1–6, 10–11; Mason, *Collection of Hymns* with Supplement (1831), sts. 1–5, 11; British Methodist *Hymns and Psalms* (1983), sts. 1–2, 4–5, 11; *United Methodist Hymnal* (1989), sts. 1–2, 4–5, 10–11.

7. All Scripture citations in this article follow the King James Version.

Even as the earliest disciples raised their voices to announce the empty tomb, so did Christ's disciples in Wesley's time raise celebratory voices to commemorate the resurrection.

STANZA 2

> Love's redeeming work is done;
> Fought the fight, the battle won;
> Lo! Our sun's eclipse is o'er;
> Lo! He sets in blood no more.

Jesus' resurrection completed his redeeming work. It is not Jesus' death alone, but his coming to life again, both born of his love, which finishes his work (Rom 6:9–11). Wesley envisioned Christ's passive suffering as an active "fight" and "battle." The mention of "our sun's eclipse" likely has a double significance. Christ's resurrection illuminates our benighted condition as people under the darkness of sin. The eclipse of line three also envisions the physical darkening described at the crucifixion of Jesus (Luke 23:45). Rather than providing a completely objective description of the resurrection ("He sets in blood no more"), Wesley included the hymn's singers as communal witnesses by using "our" rather than the definite article.

STANZA 3

> Vain the stone, the watch, the seal;
> Christ has burst the gates of hell!
> Death in vain forbids his rise:
> Christ hath open'd paradise!

Stanza three emphasizes the unstoppable power at work in Christ's resurrection by naming all opposition as "vain" in lines 1 and 3. Using itemization, and drawing on Matthew 27:66, Wesley described Pilate's futile attempts to secure the body of Jesus via the grave stone, the watch of the Roman guard, and the locking and certifying seal. Yet an even greater enemy's hold on Jesus is also "vain," for not even death, anthropomorphized here, can forbid Jesus to rise. In response to these vain oppositions, Wesley used lines 2 and 4 to declare Jesus' opening of two impossible doors. First, Christ "burst the gates of hell!" most likely referring to Christ's preaching to the imprisoned spirits (1 Pet 3:19–20) or to the famous line in the Apostles Creed, "He descended into hell."[8] The contrast with the second door in line 4 could not be

---

8. The creed would have been very familiar to Wesley as part of the daily rhythm of

greater: here Christ has "open'd paradise" (Luke 23:43). The irony is unmistakable: Pilate, backed by the power of Rome, and death, the unconquerable foe from Eden forward, are powerless to exercise their will, whereas Jesus' power is unconstrained.

STANZA 4

> Lives again our glorious King;
> Where, O death, is now thy sting?
> Dying once he all doth save;[9]
> Where thy victory, O grave?

Wesley paraphrased 1 Corinthians 15:55 in lines 2 and 4 of stanza 4 ("O death, where is thy sting? O grave, where is thy victory?").[10] Through his own resurrection, Jesus removed the sting of death and the victory of the grave for believers. The designation "glorious King" likely arises from 1 Corinthians 2:8, where Paul called Jesus the "Lord of glory."[11]

STANZA 5

> Soar we now, where Christ has led?
> Following our exalted head;
> Made like him, like him we rise;
> Ours the cross—the grave—the skies!

Stanza 5 focuses on the believer's identification with Christ. First, believers follow Christ's leading. Christ is the believer's "exalted head" (Eph 1:22). In another allusion to 1 Corinthians 15, likely verses 20 and following, Wesley noted how believers will rise like Christ himself has risen. In line 4, several key aspects of Christ's experience now become the believer's: "Ours the cross—the grave—the skies!" Wesley demonstrates a Pauline understanding of the place of the believer "in Christ."

Anglican worship.

9. Once he died our souls to save : *HSP*, eds. 4–5 (1743, 1756), MS Richmond Tracts.

10. See also Hosea 13:14, "I will ransom them from the power of the grave; I will redeem them from death: O death, I will be thy plagues; O grave, I will be thy destruction: repentance shall be hid from mine eyes."

11. Similarly, Wesley's contemporary Isaac Watts used a variant title "Prince of glory" in stanza 1 of his Communion hymn "When I survey the wondrous cross."

STANZA 6

> What tho' once we perish'd all,
> Partners in our parent's fall?
> Second life we all receive;
> In our heav'nly Adam live.

Wesley again turned to 1 Corinthians 15:22 in stanza 6, where he described the headship of Adam and of Christ: "For as in Adam all die, even so in Christ shall all be made alive." Wesley invoked a federal vision of Adam and Eve's sin and the singer's complicity in their guilt. Although all people are "partners" in "our parent's" (Adam and Eve) fall, Christ is now the believer's "heavenly Adam."

STANZA 7

> Ris'n with him, we upward move;
> Still we seek the things above;
> Still pursue, and kiss the Son,
> Seated on his Father's throne.

The seventh stanza contains at least two biblical allusions. Lines 1 and 2 reference Colossians 3:1–2: "If ye then be risen with Christ, seek those things which are above, where Christ sitteth on the right hand of God. Set your affection on things above, not on things on the earth." Paul wrote as if his recipients in Asia Minor had already experienced the resurrection; likewise, Wesley emphasized the way believers have indeed "ris'n with him." Although he wrote as if his readers were already in heaven, Paul could exhort them to "set their affections on things above." Wesley captured this exhortation: "Still we seek the things above," emphasizing the believer's ongoing pursuit of spiritual realities.[12] Lines 3 and 4 call to mind Psalm 2, especially verses 6 and 12, with their emphasis on the Son's reign and an admonition to "kiss the Son." In this stanza, Wesley noted the present reign of Christ, the believer's present-yet-unfulfilled reign with him, and the continuing worship due to the anointed Son.

STANZAS 8–9

> Scarce on earth a thought bestow;
> Dead to all we leave below;

---

12. For more on the Wesleyan view of sanctification, see Chapter 11, "Love divine, all loves excelling."

> Heav'n our aim, and lov'd abode;
> Hid our life with Christ in God!
>
> Hid, till Christ our life appear
> Glorious in his members here;
> Join'd to him, we then shall shine,
> All immortal, all divine!

Stanza 8 begins with a call to a heavenly-focused discipleship and extends the thought of the previous stanza. If Christ reigns, and believers are raised with him, they must no longer think of earthly things; they are to be dead toward that which they have "left below." For the remainder of stanza 8 and all of stanza 9, Wesley again referenced Colossians 3, this time verses 3–4: "For ye are dead, and your life is hid with Christ in God. When Christ, who is our life, shall appear, then shall ye also appear with him in glory." The eschatological movement of stanza 9 encourages believers in the present and in the future. The repetition of "hid" links stanzas 8 and 9. The believer's life is presently hidden with Christ, surely a comfort for those enduring the difficulties of a life of earthly devotion. Yet what is now hidden will one day be made visible when "Christ our life appear[s] glorious," language anticipating Christ's *parousia* and the believer's glorification ("we then shall shine").

STANZAS 10–11

> Hail the Lord of earth and heav'n!
> Praise to thee by both be giv'n;
> Thee we greet triumphant now;
> Hail the resurrection thou!
>
> King of glory, soul of bliss,
> Everlasting life is this:
> Thee to know, thy pow'r to prove,
> Thus to sing and thus to love!

Having begun the hymn with a call for believers to join heaven in celebrating the resurrection of Christ, Wesley concluded with a similar refrain. "Earth and heav'n" both praise their risen Lord, phrasing which reminds singers of Christ's present authority. The final stanza might be a reference to Paul's desire to "know [Christ] and the power of his resurrection" (Phil 3:10). For Wesley, to "know" Christ and to "prove" his power is "everlasting life." In this way, the hymn is book-ended with praise for the risen Christ.

CONCLUSION

Year after year, we might take for granted how Charles Wesley sought to honor Jesus and encourage believers through this hymn. What sort of spirituality did he hope to form within its singers? The opening and closing stanzas envelope the hymn's tone as one of celebration, not merely for the historical fact of Christ's resurrection but for its immediate and eternal impact. Believers live with comfort and power now because of their union with the risen and exalted Jesus, and this present union is the foundation of their hope for an enduring, eternal union. The breadth of theological loci within the hymn is striking, for Charles touched on areas such as Christology (sonship, resurrection, reign), hamartiology (original sin), soteriology (headship, union, glorification), and eschatology. The doctrines present here are broadly evangelical, not distinctively Methodist. Similarly striking is Wesley's familiarity with Scripture, particularly the Pauline epistles, and his ability to translate biblical texts and attendant theological concerns into the voices of eighteenth century Anglophones and beyond. The disciples' discovery, the angelic proclamation, the Colossians' hope, and Paul's desire are not merely historical concerns but present realities for those who lift their voices in song. It seems fair to characterize the hymn as soundly biblical as the words and images of Scripture abound. Through his versification, Wesley has trained generations of singers, if not the *ipsissima verba* then the *ipsissima vox* of the gospel.

Ordinances & Sanctification

9

The Means of Grace

CHRIS FENNER

Among practitioners of spiritual disciplines, the Oxford Holy Club developed one of the most rigorous regimens. The group, initiated by Charles Wesley in 1729 and supported by his brother John, included other luminaries like George Whitefield, John Clayton, and Benjamin Ingham. This society—also dubbed "the Methodists"—encouraged pious acts such as partaking Communion regularly, fasting, helping the poor, visiting the imprisoned, reading devotionally, praying, and journaling.

This rigorous lifestyle of holy living was inspired and encouraged by William Law (1686–1761). A couple of years before the Wesleys started their Holy Club, Law had published a book titled *A Practical Treatise Upon Christian Perfection* (1726), followed shortly thereafter by *A Serious Call to a Devout and Holy Life* (1729). In the latter book, Law perceived two classes of Christians:

> The one that feared and served God in the common offices and business of a secular, worldly life. The other renouncing the common business and common enjoyments of life, as riches, marriage, honours, and pleasures, devoted themselves to voluntary poverty, virginity, devotion, and retirement, that by this means they might live wholly unto God in the daily exercise of a divine and heavenly life (p. 134).

The Wesleys sought after Law's personal guidance and met with him many times to discuss these issues. But this intensive, works-oriented mindset would be turned on its ear by another influence.

A group of German Christians known as Moravians (or the United Brethren) had established connections with Protestants in England at least partly for the purpose of being included in missionary journeys to the New World, especially the Georgia colony. During one of these journeys in 1735-1736, Charles first met the Moravians, and it was through the Moravians, who were rooted in the theology of Martin Luther, that Charles and John both recognized their need for a salvation by grace alone.

And yet it was through a faction of the English Moravians that the Wesleys encountered an error opposite to their experience with Law's works-based faith. Some of their acquaintances, especially John Simpson and Philip Molther, insisted unbelievers could only come to faith by stillness, by not taking part in any Christian disciplines, in order to wait for the inspiration of the Holy Spirit. Believers, on the other hand, need not trouble themselves with outward acts or adherance to the law, because they have inward faith. This latter belief is called *antinomianism*.

In response to both poles—justification by works on the one side, and freedom from works on the other—John and Charles crafted an important and careful response, John via a sermon, and Charles via a hymn, both titled "The Means of Grace." For his sermon,[1] John pointed first and foremost to Malachi 3:7, "Ye are gone away from mine ordinances, and have not kept them." In addressing the stillness movement, he reminded readers, "Christ had ordained certain outward means for conveying his grace into the souls of men. Their constant practice set this beyond all dispute; for so long as 'all that believed were together, and had all things in common (Acts 2:44), they continued steadfastly in the teaching of the Apostles, and in the breaking of bread and in prayers (v. 42).'" In addressing his own background in works-based righteousness, he said, "But in the process of time, when 'the love of many waxed cold' [Matt 24:12], some began to mistake the means for an end, and to place religion, rather in doing those outward works, than in a heart renewed after the image of God."

The hymn Charles crafted, first published as a pamphlet in April of 1740 then included in *Hymns and Sacred Poems* later that July,[2] master-

---

1. John Wesley, "The Means of Grace," 1:225-250.

2. Maddox, *Means of Grace*, in *Charles Wesley's Published Verse*. The hymn was Included in *Hymns and Sacred Poems* [HSP] (1740), then repeated in *Hymns and Spiritual Songs* [HSS], in 24 eds. (1753-1786), reduced to 10 sts. beginning "Suffice for me," etc., with other changes. In *A Collection of Hymns for the Use of the People Called Methodists* (1780), this was given in 8 stanzas, including 1-2, 6, 3-5, 7, and 16 of the original, with

fully addressed both sides, guiding readers to a proper understanding of ritual and faith, while also speaking from a position of personal testimony. The complete text spans 23 stanzas:

> Long have I seem'd to serve Thee, Lord,
>   With unavailing pain;
> Fasted, and pray'd, and read Thy Word,
>   And heard it preach'd, in vain.
>
> Oft did I with th' assembly join,
>   And near Thine[3] alter drew;
> A form of godliness was mine,
>   The pow'r I never knew.
>
> To please Thee thus, at length[4] I see,
>   Vainly[5] I hoped, and strove:
> For what are outward things to Thee,
>   Unless they spring from love?
>
> I see the perfect law requires
>   Truth in the inward parts,
> Our full consent, our whole desires,[6]
>   Our undivided hearts.
>
> But I of means have made my boast,
>   Of means an idol made!
> The spirit in the letter lost,
>   The substance in the shade!
>
> I rested in the outward law,
>   Nor knew its deep design;
> The length and breadth I never saw,
>   And height of love divine.
>
> Where am I now, or what my hope?
>   What can my weakness do?
> Jesu![7] to Thee my soul looks up,
>   'Tis Thou must make it new.
>
> Thine is the work, and Thine alone—

---

some changes; in the 2nd ed. and following, the last stanza (16) was omitted.

3. thy : *Collection* (1780).
4. as last : *HSP* (1740).
5. In vain : *HSP* (1740).
6. desire : *Collection*, 1st ed. only (1780).
7. I err, : *Collection*, 1st ed. only (1780).

But shall I idly stand?
Shall I the written rule disown
    And slight my God's command?

Wildly shall I from Thine turn back,
    A better path to find;
Thy holy ordinance forsake,
    And cast Thy words behind?

Forbid it, gracious Lord, that I
    Should ever learn Thee so!
No—let me with Thy Word comply,
    If I Thy love would know.

Suffice for me, that Thou, my Lord,
    Hast bid me fast and pray:
Thy will be done, Thy name ador'd;
    'Tis only mine t'obey.

Thou bid'st me search the sacred leaves
    And taste the hallow'd bread;
The kind command[8] my soul receives,
    And longs on Thee to feed.

Still for Thy loving kindness, Lord,
    I in Thy temple wait,
I long[9] to find Thee in Thy Word,
    Or at Thy table meet.

Here, in Thine own appointed ways,
    I wait to learn Thy will;
Silent I stand before Thy face,
    And hear Thee say, "Be still!"

"Be still—and know that I am God!"
    'Tis all I live to know,
To feel the virtue of Thy blood
    And spread its praise below.

I wait my vigour to renew,
    Thine image to retrieve;
The veil of outward things pass through,
    And gasp in Thee to live.

I work, and own the labour vain,

---

8. commands : *HSP* (1740), *HSS*, 1st ed. (1753).
9. look : *HSP* (1740).

And thus from works I cease;
I strive and see my fruitless pain,
    Till God create my peace.

Fruitless, till Thou Thyself impart,
    Must all my efforts prove:
They cannot change a sinful heart;
    They cannot purchase love.

I do the thing Thy laws enjoin,
    And then the strife give o'er;
To Thee I then the whole resign;
    I trust in means no more.

I trust in Him who stands between
    The Father's wrath and me:
Jesu! Thou great eternal mean,
    I look for all from Thee.

Thy mercy pleads, Thy truth requires,
    Thy promise calls Thee down;
Not for the sake of my desires—
    But oh! regard Thine own!

I seek no motive out of Thee;
    Thine own desires fulfill;
If now thy bowels yearn on me,
    On me perform Thy will.

Doom, if Thou canst, to endless pains,
    And drive me from Thy face,[10]
But if Thy stronger love constrains,
    Let me be sav'd by grace.

The first seven stanzas grow out of Wesley's own personal experience, of reaching a place where he was able to ask, "For what are outward things to Thee, unless they spring from love?" The next five stanzas establish the other

---

10. In Maddox's edition of *HSP* (1740), he noted the inclusion of these two lines in a debate between Thomas Church and John Wesley. In Church's complaint, issued as *Remarks on the Reverend Mr. John Wesley's Last Journal* (1745), he charged Wesley with believing Christians don't suffer on earth, an error he called "A stoical insensibility." He saw this partly in the lines of this hymn, where "you seem to carry this notion, to the very height of extravagance and presumption" (pp. 58–59). Wesley defended himself in *An Answer to the Rev. Mr. Church's Remarks* (1745), in which he clarified the conditional phrase, "if thou canst": "If thou canst deny thyself, if thou canst forget to be gracious, if thou canst cease to be Truth and Love. So the lines both preceding and following fix the sense. I see nothing of stoical insensibility, neither of extravagancy or presumption in this" (p. 37).

side of spiritual balance: a reminder of how all those outward acts—fasting, prayer, reading Scripture, taking Communion—are still part of God's commands. Wesley then turned his attention to confronting the antinomianism of his peers and shaping a proper concept of what it means to be spiritually still: "Here, in Thine own appointed ways, I wait to learn Thy will; silent I stand before Thy face, and hear Thee say, 'Be still!'" Those appointed ways, Wesley wrote, meant seeking the Lord in his temple, in his Word, and at his table. To close the hymn, Wesley cycled back to his original point. The spiritual disciplines, although good and necessary, "cannot change a sinful heart, they cannot purchase love." If God's sovereign love should allow it, "Let me be sav'd by grace."

In this manner, Wesley was able to smartly navigate the waters between Isaiah 1, where God condemns external ritual if it is done with corrupt hearts, and James 2, where "faith by itself, if it does not have works, is dead." This is a hymn worth dissecting for any pastor, teacher, student, disciple, or congregation seeking to understand the law, the ordinances, and spiritual disciplines, assessed in light of a salvation justified by grace alone and made possible only by the work of Christ.[11]

---

11. A shorter version of this article appeared in *Towers*, The Southern Baptist Theological Seminary 14/8 (April 2016) 20.

10

O the depth of love divine

Paul W. Chilcote

The movement of spiritual renewal within the Church of England, in which Charles Wesley figured so prominently alongside his brother John, was a sacramental as well as an evangelical revival. Both brothers embraced a robust Eucharistic spirituality and reclaimed the central place of the Sacrament in the Christian journey of faith among the various means of grace.[1] Contemporaries knew the Methodists by two distinguishing marks—their singing and their "constant Communion." The hymns of Charles Wesley fueled this Eucharistic revival and shaped Methodist theology. In 1745, the brothers jointly published a collection of *Hymns on the Lord's Supper* for the use of Methodists during the distribution of the sacramental elements and at other appropriate times of worship and devotion. One of the hymns from this collection, "O the depth of love divine," provides a window into Charles's lyrical theology of the Sacrament.[2]

---

1. On Charles Wesley's Eucharistic theology, see Rattenbury, *Eucharistic Hymns*, and Stevick, *The Altar's Fire*.

2. I have discussed Wesley's Eucharistic theology in a chapter entitled "Communion: Spiritual Food for the Journey," in my book, *A Faith That Sings*, 90–105. Some of the material here depends on this earlier work. See also Chilcote, "John and Charles Wesley," in *Christian Theologies*, 272–94.

CHARLES WESLEY AND THE "RICHEST LEGACY"

As a devout Anglican priest, Charles defined a sacrament on the basis of the Church of England *Catechism* as "an outward sign of inward *grace*, and a *means* whereby we receive the same."[3] Article XVI, "Of the Sacraments," from the Anglican *Articles of Religion*, also shaped his thinking in this regard.[4] Through the Sacrament, the Wesleys believed God not only works within the believer invisibly (conversion), but also strengthens the recipient in his or her faith (confirmation). Eucharist functions not only as a confirming ordinance; it is also a "converting ordinance."[5] It is not surprising, then, that Charles described the Sacrament of Holy Communion as the "richest legacy" Jesus left the community of faith.

> This is the richest legacy
>   Thou hast on man bestow'd;
> Here chiefly, Lord, we feed on thee,
>   And drink thy precious blood.[6]

During his second year of studies at Oxford University, having somewhat frittered away his inaugural year, Charles resolved to change. "I set myself to serious thinking," he acknowledged. "I went to the weekly sacrament, and persuaded two or three young scholars to accompany me."[7] So began his life-long devotion to the Sacrament, a practice he modeled for the people called Methodists. Concerning his influence and that of his brother on their followers in this regard, John Bowmer observed:

> There can be little doubt that the high place which the Sacrament occupied in early Methodism was due to the precept and the example of the Wesleys, for it is not too much to say that, for them it was the highest form of devotion and the most comprehensive act of worship the Church could offer. As necessary as preaching was—and it would be unjust to attempt to minimize

---

3. See Baker et al., *Works of John Wesley*, 1:381, from John Wesley's sermon "The Means of Grace (II.1)." St. Augustine coined the classic expression: "an outward and visible sign of an inward and spiritual grace."

4. See John Wesley, *Sunday Service of the Methodists*, 311. John reproduced this Article from the *Book of Common Prayer* (1662) nearly verbatim.

5. John Wesley's journal for 27–28 June 1740, in Baker et al., *Works of John Wesley*, 19:158–159.

6. Charles Wesley, "Glory to Him who freely spent," in *Hymns on the Lord's Supper*, 31 (Hymn 42, st. 4). All hymn texts throughout this chapter cite Wesley's first editions, as compiled by Maddox, *Charles Wesley's Published Verse*.

7. Charles Wesley, letter to Dr. Chandler, 28 April 1785, in Tyson, *Charles Wesley: A Reader*, 59.

its place in the Methodist revival—a preaching service was not, to the Wesleys, the supreme spiritual exercise. On the other hand, the Lord's Supper was completely satisfying.[8]

Early Methodists flocked to the celebration of Holy Communion because they encountered God there. They received spiritual nourishment around the table. Locating the Sacrament among other means of grace, Charles Wesley sang:

> The prayer, the fast, the word conveys,
>   When mixt with faith, thy life to me,
> In all the channels of thy grace,
>   I still have fellowship with thee,
> But chiefly here my soul is fed
> With fullness of immortal bread.[9]

The singing of these hymns not only influenced the sacramental practice of the Methodists but also shaped their understanding of God's love for them and their reciprocal love for God.

CHARLES WESLEY'S HYMNS ON THE LORD'S SUPPER

Although the Wesley brothers jointly published *Hymns on the Lord's Supper* (1745), Charles wrote all 166 hymns in this unique volume.[10] This collection comprised the fullest possible expression of his Eucharistic spirituality. The publication included an abridged version of Daniel Brevint's *The Christian Sacrament and Sacrifice* (1673), which functioned as a preface to the volume. The hymns were arranged under primary headings, closely following the pattern laid out by Brevint in his treatise:

1. As it is a Memorial of the Sufferings and Death of Christ.
2. As it is a Sign and a Means of Grace.
3. The Sacrament a Pledge of Heaven.
4. The Holy Eucharist as it implies a Sacrifice.
5. Concerning the Sacrifice of our Persons.
6. After the Sacrament.

8. Bowmer, *Sacrament of the Lord's Supper*, 188–89.
9. Wesley, *Hymns on the Lord's Supper*, 39 (Hymn 54, st. 4).
10. This collection of hymns went through nine editions during the lifetime of the brothers and was one of their primary means to revive the Eucharistic life of the Church of England.

The first three sections closely parallel the dimensions of time and provide the outline for Charles's lyrical theological reflections on the sacrament. First, the Lord's Supper is a memorial of the passion of Christ (the past dimension and love). Second, the Eucharist is a celebration of the presence of the living Christ (the present dimension and faith). Third, Holy Communion is a pledge of the heavenly banquet to come (the future dimension and hope). But the Sacrament also implies a sacrifice, and the hymns of the final sections refer not only to the dynamic sacrifice of Christ, but remind the community of faithful disciples about their obligation to engage in self-sacrificing acts of love in imitation of Christ.

Charles employed these various dimensions and images in an effort to communicate the depth and breadth of meaning in the Sacrament and to enrich the experience of the participants. In this sign-act of love, the past, present, and future—faith, hope, and love—are compressed, as it were, into a timeless, communal act of praise. He celebrated the fullness of the Christian faith in the mystery of a holy meal, in which the people of God are empowered to faithful ministry and service. As faithful disciples repeatedly participate in the Eucharistic actions of taking, blessing, breaking, and giving—the constitutive aspects of an authentic, sacrificial life—God conforms them to the image of Christ.

AN EXPLICATION OF THE HOLY MYSTERY

The hymn "O the depth of love divine" is number 57, in section II, in which Wesley included texts describing the Sacrament "As it is a Sign and Means of Grace." This hymn reflects three particular aspects of Charles Wesley's lyrical theology of the Eucharist: presence, power, and perfection.

Presence. Wesley never feared to ask difficult questions in his hymns. His text begins with questions, age-old questions with which the church has struggled long, about the presence of God in the Sacrament.

> O the depth of love divine,
> > Th' unfathomable grace!
> Who shall say how bread and wine
> > God into man conveys?
> *How* the bread his flesh imparts,
> > *How* the wine transmits his blood,
> Fills his faithful people's hearts
> > With all the life of God!

Reflecting on this opening stanza of the hymn, S.T. Kimbrough wrote, Charles "is laying before the church and followers of Christ in all ages the awesomeness of the divine wisdom which resides in and is imparted by sharing the common table with one another and with Christ."[11] The first line establishes the main point: "the depth of love divine" made known to us through an incomprehensible grace. Despite the mystery articulated in the questions, the Sacrament, according to Wesley, effects what it represents. According to Rattenbury, "an examination of the hymns will result quite frequently in the discovery of allusions to the 'real Presence' of Christ, but it is always a *personal* Presence."[12] Ole Borgen described this Wesleyan concept of real presence as a dynamic or living presence, affirming, "where God acts, there he is."[13]

Power. Charles declared the depths of this holy mystery—something lying beyond the possibility of rational explanation—in the second and third stanzas, where he also introduced the concept of virtue or power:

> Let the wisest mortal show
> > How we the grace receive;
> Feeble elements bestow
> > A power not theirs to give:
> Who explains the wondrous way?
> > How thro' these the virtue came?
> These the virtue did convey,
> > Yet still remain the same.
>
> How can heavenly spirits rise
> > By earthly matter fed,
> Drink herewith divine supplys
> > And eat immortal bread?
> Ask the Father's wisdom *how*;
> > Him that did the means ordain
> Angels round our altars bow
> > To search it out, in vain.

Wesley believed the Sacrament is made effective through the power of the Holy Spirit. This is what he meant in his use of the term "virtue." The "elements bestow / A power not theirs to give." Yet, through the elements, he affirms the virtue has come; the elements convey the virtue—the power—to the recipient. "The 'objective presence' cannot be thought of as the static presence of an object," observed Bishop Borgen, "but rather as that

---

11. Kimbrough, *A Heart to Praise My God*, 148.
12. Rattenbury, *Eucharistic Hymns*, 59.
13. Borgen, *Wesley on the Sacraments*, 69.

of a living and acting person *working* through the means."[14] Or as David Stevick has written, "The readiest equivalent for 'virtue' would be 'power,' an idea which is sometimes present in lines where the term 'virtue' is not used.... Divine power is divine reality.... The bread and wine are essential conveyances of divine life, but the wonder is that they are so while remaining bread and wine (57:2.7–8)."[15]

Perfection. Wesley concluded his hymn with a bold affirmation:

> Sure and real is the grace,
>   The manner be unknown;
> Only meet us in thy ways
>   And perfect us in one,
> Let us taste the heavenly powers,
>   Lord, we ask for nothing more;
> Thine to bless, 'tis only ours
>   To wonder, and adore.

Despite the fact we cannot define or even describe the manner in which God offers grace to us in the Sacrament, the means, the grace, the power of this love is real. Charles used the verb "perfect" here. "Only meet us in thy ways / And perfect us in one." He employed this kind of language frequently, and it signals to us that something of supreme importance attaches to this practice and what it conveys. He refers here, in fact, to the process by which the Spirit makes the child of God more and more like Jesus. On its most basic level, for Wesley the verb "perfect" means to be made holy.[16]

He almost always defined this holiness with reference to the two great commandments of Jesus, the twin dimensions of sanctification: holiness of heart, or love of God, and holiness of life, or love of neighbor (Matt 22:37–39). He was not only concerned about people experiencing forgiveness for sin (justification), he also wanted them to move toward the fullest possible wholeness and healing as well (sanctification). Faith, in his view, leads to love in the Christian life, and to be loving or holy is to be truly happy. But note how he framed this perfection here in the plural: "perfect *us* in one." Only the fullest possible love has the power to unify the community of faith. Wesley's petition here, as S.T. Kimbrough has noted, "indicates that the church's sign of the means of grace is perfect unity. Unity in the community of faith signals the world that it is a recipient and instrument of God's grace."[17] Eucharistic practice, in other words, has the power to shape the community of faith into

---

14. Borgen, *John Wesley on the Sacraments*, 69.
15. Stevick, *The Altar's Fire: Charles Wesley's*, 33.
16. See Chilcote, "All the image of Thy love," 21–40.
17. Kimbrough, *A Heart to Praise*, 149.

a unified body of faithful witnesses to God's love in the world. So for Wesley, the people of God move from the table into God's world, in mission until God restores all and everyone is left "to wonder, and adore."

11

Love divine, all loves excelling

ROGER D. DUKE & CHRIS FENNER

In the development of Methodism, John and Charles recognized the importance of using hymns to carry doctrinal messages; their extensive publishing venture was vital in that role. Since congregational singing can be used to teach basic tenets of the Christian faith, "The Wesleys understood . . . their hymnals to be handbooks of doctrine."[1] In many cases, they published small collections focused on particular themes.

In 1747, the Wesleys released *Hymns for Those that Seek and Those that Have Redemption in the Blood of Jesus Christ*, containing 52 hymn texts. Each text referred in some way to matters of salvation. The first 24 hymns were designed to coordinate with the tunes in *Hymns on the Great Festivals* (1746). One editor of the Wesleys' hymns, Randy Maddox, described the collection as "the work of [Charles] Wesley as a 'practical theologian,' charting a narrative for the spiritual journey of those reading and singing the verse."[2] Wesley scholar John Tyson saw this collection as extending the Wesleys' ongoing concern for holiness, asserting, "these compositions explore what sanctification looks like in everyday life."[3]

The most enduring of these hymns has been "Love divine, all loves excelling."[4] As hymn number nine, it was intended to be sung to the tune

1. Knight, "Wesley and the Doctrinal Role of Hymnody," in *Catalyst*.
2. Maddox, *Redemption Hymns* (1747), in *Charles Wesley's Manuscript Verse*.
3. Tyson, *Assist Me to Proclaim*, 240.
4. Maddox lists two manuscript precursors of this hymn, MS Shent (MA 1977/554)

corresponding to "Jesus, show us thy salvation" in *Hymns on the Great Festivals*, a rather ambitious melody by John Frederick Lampe (1703–1751).

STANZA 1

> Love divine, all loves excelling,
>   Joy of heaven, to earth come down,[5]
> Fix in us thy humble dwelling,
>   All thy faithful mercies crown;
> Jesu, Thou art all compassion,
>   Pure unbounded love Thou art;
> Visit us with thy salvation,
>   Enter every trembling heart.

The opening lines of the hymn were an imitation of a song from the opera *King Arthur*, Act II, Scene 5, words by John Dryden (1631–1700), with music by Henry Purcell (1659–1695):

> Fairest Isle, all isles excelling,
> Seat of pleasures, and of loves;
> Venus here will choose her dwelling,
> And forsake her Cyprian groves.

Hymnologist J.R. Watson described the relationship between the two: "Wesley characteristically takes over a classical reference and makes a Christian point: instead of Venus, the goddess of love, leaving Cyprus for the British Isles, Divine Love is to leave heaven and dwell in the human heart."[6] When this hymn appeared again in *Select Hymns with Tunes Annext* (1761), the connection to *King Arthur* was even more deliberate. Instead of being paired with Lampe's tune from 1746, this text was printed with Purcell's opera tune.[7]

94a–94b, and MS Thirty (MA 1977/424) 135–36; both are held at the Methodist Archive and Research Centre, University of Manchester, and they were transcribed by Maddox for *Charles Wesley's Manuscript Verse*.

5. Baker et al., *Works of John Wesley*, 7:545: "The original comma rather than a semicolon at the end of the line showed that this was a declaration of faith rather than a prayer, and this was emphasized by the addition of a comma after 'heaven' in the 1779 edn. of *Redemption H*. In the edns. of the *Collection* the semicolon first appeared in [the 7th edn.], 1791. Wesley's MS draft, however, 1778, reads: 'Joy of heaven, to earth come down!'"

6. Watson, *Annotated Anthology of Hymns*, 196. Watson also sees parallels with Ovid's *Metamorphoses*, "because Ovid's poem deals with change and transformation, . . . but also because there is a particular story of divinities coming to earth" in Book VIII.

7. In *Select Hymns with Tunes Annext* (1761), no. 128, Purcell's tune was called WESTMINSTER. It had been adapted as a hymn tune for Methodists seven years earlier in *The Divine Musical Miscellany* (1754), a tunebook for use with George Whitefield's

The first stanza serves as an invocation to the rest of the hymn. It is a five-fold prayer to Christ. Because God's divine love excels all other affections humanly known, Wesley called on Christ to "come," "fix," "crown," "visit," and "enter ev'ry trembling heart."[8] Without a doubt—based on the Wesleyan body of divinity—Charles longed for this deeper "love divine" relationship with the Master. This love could be known corporately by the church, but Wesley desired for all to experience it personally and intimately. The hymn-prayer has a basis in Christ's Incarnation: when Christ comes experientially, the joy of heaven has come to earth (John 1:14), He has fixed in us His humble home (John 14:23), He has crowned us with His mercies (2 Tim 4:8),[9] He has visited us with His salvation (Ps 106:4),[10] and He shall enter every trembling heart (2 Cor 4:6, Eph 3:17–19).

Note the descriptors Wesley applied to Christ. He called Him the "joy of heaven," "all compassion," and "pure unbounded love." The call for Christ to make His humble dwelling in us is an appeal to another title, Immanuel, God-with-us (Isa 7:14, Matt 1:23), another connection to the Incarnation. The significance of his description shows a progression of thought and theology: Christ was full of unbounded love, He possessed all compassion, and He brought down the joy of heaven. That joy of heaven was Christ himself! From transcendence to immanence; from the Father's right hand, to "be made in the likeness of men, He humbled himself and became obedient unto death, even the death of the cross" (Phil 2:7–8). Christ himself, Christ's Incarnation, Christ come down, Christ's presence with us is "Love divine, all loves excelling."

STANZA 2

> Breathe, O breathe thy loving Spirit
> Into every troubled breast;
> Let us all in Thee inherit,
> Let us find that second rest;
> Take away our power of sinning,
> Alpha and Omega be,
> End of faith as its beginning,
> Set our hearts at liberty.

Hymns for Social Worship (1753).

8. Bailey, *Gospel in Hymns*, 96.

9. See also James 1:12, 1 Peter 5:4, and Revelation 2:10.

10. See especially the KJV, "Remember me, O Lord, with the favour that thou bearest unto thy people: O visit me with thy salvation."

The attitude of prayer continues here, asking that "certain longed-for results shall follow the indwelling Spirit of love: trouble relieved, rest secured, the desire to sin removed, release from the bondage of sin."[11] The Spirit will perform dynamics for and in the believer. The Spirit's breathing on the believer references Christ, when he "breathed on them and said unto them, receive ye the Holy Ghost" (John 20:22). The stanza ends with "Alpha and Omega be" (Rev 22:13) and "End of faith as its beginning" (Heb 12:2), biblical allusions to the finished work of Christ. But the Holy Spirit's "office work" in the believer is Wesley's main emphasis in this second stanza.

The fourth and fifth lines, regarding the "second rest" and the "power of sinning," require special consideration. These lines have been the most controversial, even in the lifetimes of John and Charles, and even between the brothers. These lines draw from their beliefs about Christian perfection (sanctification), based to some degree on the works of William Law (1686–1761)[12] and on passages such as Matthew 5:48, "Be ye therefore perfect, even as your Father which is in heaven is perfect" (KJV). In his journal for September 26, 1740, Charles offered this description of Christian perfection: "utter dominion over sin; constant peace, and love, and joy in the Holy Ghost; the full assurance of faith, righteousness, and true holiness."[13] For Charles, the attainment of perfection should be marked by humility and complete dependence on Christ. In 1741, he wrote a hymn called "The Promise of Sanctification," published together with John's sermon "Christian Perfection,"[14] in which Charles described an inverse relationship:

> Now let me gain perfection's height!
>   Now let me into nothing fall!
> Be less than nothing in thy sight,
>   And feel that Christ is all in all.

Over time, the disagreement between the brothers became a matter of whether and how Christian perfection could be attained on this side of heaven. The issue came to a head around 1760, when several people in their circle of influence claimed to have been completely delivered from sin. Whereas John was inclined to believe these testimonies, Charles was not. Charles had come to believe complete sanctification only happened on the other side of death. The difference between the two was expressed by John in a letter to Charles, July 9, 1764: "That perfection which I believe, I can

---

11. Bailey, *The Gospel in Hymns*, 96.

12. Especially Law's *Practical Treatise upon Christian Perfection* (1726). See also Chapter 9 in this volume, "The Means of Grace."

13. Kimbrough and Newport, *Manuscript Journal*, 1:279.

14. John Wesley, *Christian Perfection: A Sermon* (1741).

boldly preach, because I think I see five hundred witnesses of it. Of that perfection which you preach, you do not even see any witnesses at all."[15]

This distinction also played out in the printing of this hymn. In 1761, when tension between the brothers was high, they each produced their own hymnals. John compiled *Select Hymns with Tunes Annext*, in which "Love divine" was printed in full, unchanged from 1747. Charles compiled *Hymns for Those to Whom Christ is All in All*, in which "Love divine" was reduced to three stanzas, minus this second stanza about Christian perfection. Notice also the connection between the title and Charles's earlier hymn. As Wesley editor Randy Maddox put it, "Charles's concern about the perfectionist controversy is likely what led him to publish [the 1761 volume]. . . . He considered verbal claims to perfection to be vain boasting, maintaining that the truly perfect would testify only of their dependence upon Christ."[16]

STANZA 3

> Come, Almighty to deliver,
> Let us all thy life receive,
> Suddenly return, and never,
> Never more thy temples leave.
> Thee we would be always blessing,
> Serve thee as thy host above,
> Pray, and praise thee without ceasing,
> Glory in thy perfect love.

The focus of stanza 3 is a "desire never to be separated from the presence of God, either in time or eternity."[17] In his continued plea, Wesley invoked an Old Testament name for God, "Almighty," but here he applied it to the second-coming Christ. He prayed for deliverance. Wesley longed for the Almighty's sudden return; the appeal is for Christ to "never, never more thy temples leave." In the New Testament, we understand the true temples to

---

15. Tyson, *Charles Wesley: A Reader*, 384.

16. Maddox, *All in All* (1761), in *Charles Wesley's Published Verse*. For more background on the perfection issue, see also Tyson, *Assist Me to Proclaim*, 230–251; Baker et al., *Works of John Wesley*, 7:16–19, 545–574; Kimbrough, *Lyrical Theology*, 88–91, frames this discussion around the term *theosis*; and Lawson, *A Thousand Tongues*, 193–195. Lawson saw the phrase "Take away our power of sinning" as a reference to St. Augustine, *De civitate Dei*, xxii:30, "The first immortality, which Adam lost by sinning, was the ability not to die (*posse non mori*), the new immortality will be the inability to die (*non posse mori*). In the same way, the first freedom of choice conveyed the ability not to sin (*posse non peccare*); the new freedom will confer the inability to sin (*non posse peccare*)."

17. Bailey, *The Gospel in Hymns*, 96.

be the bodies of believers (1 Cor 6:19); in this sense, Wesley was following the petition of stanza 1, to "enter ev'ry trembling heart," and stanza 2, to "breathe thy loving Spirit into every troubled breast," then never remove His physical presence from believers.

There is a marked shift in the second half of the stanza: when the Almighty does return, the scene changes from deliverance to worship. God will always be with His people, both as their deliverer and as their object of worship. Images from Revelation are in view, especially Revelation 21:3, "Behold, the tabernacle of God is with men, and He shall dwell with them, and they shall be his people, and God himself shall be with them, and be their God" (KJV).[18] Rehearse Wesley's words as he describes the Church's eternal worship: "Thee we would be always blessing, serve thee as thy hosts above, pray and praise thee without ceasing, glory in thy perfect love." Wesley's hymn echoes the cry of John the Revelator, "Even so, come, Lord Jesus" (Rev 22:20).

STANZA 4

> Finish then thy new creation,
>   Pure and sinless let us be,
> Let us see thy great salvation,
>   Perfectly restored in thee;
> Changed from glory into glory,
>   Till in heav'n we take our place,
> Till we cast our crowns before thee,
>   Lost in wonder, love, and praise.

Stanza 4 is a continuation of the eschatological vision of the previous stanza. Here also two divisions are seen in the text: the first four lines describe what is done in the believer, and the last four point to the ultimate worship to occur in Heaven.

First, Wesley longed for the "new creation" begun at the rebirth, brought to fruition in every believer. The concern for Christian perfection emerges again here—"pure and sinless let us be"—except here it is attached to heavenly glorification, as it should be. The poetry then connects the internal and personal work of holiness with the universal greatness of God's salvation. In the text, Wesley yearned for the heavenly fulfillment of the partial sanctification he had known on earth, when he would be "perfectly restored." All in all, for Charles Wesley, Heaven would be the perfect manifestation of the divine love he had sought and experienced his entire earthly life.

---

18. See also Revelation, chapters 5, 21, and 22.

Second, Wesley turned from the micro-work of Christ in each believer to the macro-worship of Christ in eternity. "Changed from glory into glory" recalls the Apostle Paul's declaration in 2 Corinthians 3:18, "But we all, with open face beholding as in a glass the glory of the Lord, are changed into the same image from glory to glory, even as by the Spirit of the Lord" (KJV). Wesley's hymn looks forward to this, when all the redeemed will be where they are supposed to be. And all the redeemed will be rightly employed for the work for which God has chosen them—worship, casting our crowns before the Messiah (Rev 4:10). Then and then alone, in the eschaton, will we know what it means to be "Lost in wonder, love, and praise." This last line was borrowed from a hymn by Joseph Addison (1672–1719), whose work was known to the Wesleys:

> When all thy mercies, O my God,
>   My rising soul surveys,
> Transported with the view, I'm lost
>   In wonder, love, and praise.[19]

CODA

Near the end of their lives and ministries, John assembled *A Collection of Hymns for the Use of the People Called Methodists* (1780). To him it was the summation of all the central doctrines pertaining to Methodism. John stated in the introduction, "It is large enough to contain all the important truths of our most holy religion, whether speculative or practical; yea, to illustrate them all, and to prove them both by Scripture and reason."[20] The role of such a hymnal was (and still is) vital for the instruction of basic tenets of the Christian faith via song. Many might not participate in the catechism, but they can learn doctrine by singing godly hymns. Wesleyan scholar Henry H. Knight III described the role of this collection in the context of early Methodism:

> Just as the Articles of Religion, Book of Homilies, and Book of Common Prayer provided theological grounding for the Church of England, the hymns joined J. Wesley's sermons, commentaries, and conference minutes as means to convey Wesleyan theology. Their purpose was not to serve as an "official" doctrinal authority but to disseminate the theology to the widest possible audience.[21]

---

19. Addison, *The Spectator*, 317. The Wesleys included this in *A Collection of Psalms and Hymns* (1737), no. XXVII.

20. Wesley, *Collection*, iv.

21. Knight, "Wesley and the Doctrinal Role of Hymnody," in *Catalyst*.

The hymns were carefully organized into pedagogic categories like a catechetical tool would be. John explained, "The hymns are not carelessly jumbled together, but carefully [ar]ranged under their proper heads, according to the experience of real Christians. So this book is in effect a little body of experimental and practical divinity."[22]

Among the hymns in this collection was "Love divine, all loves excelling," placed in the organizational scheme under Section VII: Groaning for Full Redemption. Here, John followed his brother's example from 1761 and omitted the second stanza. At the same time, he introduced two small changes. "Let us all thy life receive" became "Let us all thy grace receive," a change hymnologist J.R. Watson felt was unfortunate, or "less apposite to the Incarnational theology of the hymn as a whole. . . . Charles Wesley's precision of thought is well seen in 'life' (from John 10:10, 'I am come that they may have life, and have it more abundantly')."[23] The other change is a further response to the issue of Christian perfection, altered from the original "Pure and sinless let us be" to "Pure and spotless let us be," which accords nicely with the description of sanctification in Ephesians 5:27 ("a glorious church, not having spot or wrinkle," KJV).

Some hymnal compilers have reclaimed or preserved the second stanza, with some adjustments. Martin Madan (1726–1790), friend and colleague of the Wesleys, was the first to employ "Let us find thy promised rest,"[24] an example many others have followed. He also possibly influenced John's later editorial work by offering "Pure, unspotted may we be." Augustus Toplady (1740–1778), who had his fair share of theological disagreements with the Wesleys, wasn't opposed to using this hymn. He repeated Madan's "promised rest," introduced "Take away the love of sinning," an alteration many others have repeated, and printed "Pure and holy may we be," among other changes.[25]

One thing is certain, hymn singing was vital to the growth of the evangelical movement led by the Wesleys and their fellow Methodists. As one writer expressed it, the hymns were important for the Wesleys as "a means of expressing joy and teaching scriptural truth."[26] Their hymns have continued to teach and enrich countless generations of worshipers. How full our worship is because of "O for a thousand tongues to sing," "Rejoice, the Lord is King," "Jesu, lover of my soul," "Christ the Lord is ris'n today," and "Hark,

22. Wesley, *Collection*, iv.
23. Watson, *Annotated Anthology*, 197.
24. Madan, *Collection of Psalms and Hymns*, no. XLIX.
25. Toplady, *Psalms and Hymns*, no. XCVIII.
26. Severance, "Charles Wesley," in *Christianity.com*.

the herald angels sing." Truly, "Love divine, all loves excelling"—with its literary heritage, its scriptural depth, its poetic craftsmanship, and its doctrinal richness—causes the cup of worship to overflow.

A Prayer of Evangelism

12

Sun of unclouded righteousness

MICHAEL A.G. HAYKIN

While contemporary occidental perceptions of Islam are derived from a variety of media, earlier eras were far more limited as to the number of sources about this religion. In the eighteenth century, for example, European print culture was the major—and for many, the sole—medium by which western thinking about Muslims and their beliefs was shaped. And in the British Isles, one book in particular stands out as key to understanding the way Islam was viewed by the British of this era, namely, *The True Nature of Imposture Fully Display'd in the Life of Mahomet* (1697) by Humphrey Prideaux (1648–1724), Dean of Norwich for the last twenty-two years of his life. Viewed as a clear and learned author,[1] Prideaux's work went through seven editions in twenty years and became a standard interpretation of Muhammad (c.570–632) and the religion he founded in the early Enlightenment.[2]

Prideaux had intended this work to be part of a much larger volume tracing the decline of Eastern Christendom in the three centuries following the rise of Islam and the way in which bitter theological divisions had rent the churches of the East and had consequently contributed to their ruin at the hands of Muslims.[3] In the 1690s, though, there had appeared a number of Deist works rooted in a rationalistic temper of mind, critical of all religious arguments based on divine revelation. Prideaux reckoned the

---

1. Darling, *Cyclopaedia Bibliographica*, 2450.
2. Almond, "Western Images of Islam, 1700–1900," 412–413.
3. Prideaux, *True Nature*, v–xi.

deleterious impact of these works would not have been as great if it had not been attended by a "giddy Humour" which especially gripped younger church leaders in England of "following whatsoever hath gotten into fashion and vogue."[4] Lest he give these opponents of Christianity ammunition for their attacks, Prideaux decided to make his biography of Muhammad part of an overall response to Deism, in which he would show, by way of Muhammad's beliefs and life, the marks of a fraudulent religion and why such marks were not a part of the Christian Faith.[5]

Prideaux's work would be remembered and prized in the following century not so much for his refutation of the Deists as for his polemical portrayal of Muhammad as an "impostor," even though there were definite flaws apparent in his biographical account.[6] One eighteenth-century reader who was especially critical of his study was his French contemporary, Henri, Comte de Boulainvilliers (1658-1722), whose own life of Muhammad was published posthumously in 1730. Boulainvilliers was prepared to admit Prideaux was "a very judicious historian," but he took issue with his presentation of Muhammad as "an impostor, as ignorant as contemptible."[7] Rather, Boulainvilliers believed the origins of Islam lay in noble, though misguided, motives: "the intellectual love of an invisible object," namely God, and "a zeal to procure him some sort of new adoration, an ardour to combat tenets . . . thought erroneous, and above all, an imagination heated with rapid ideas."[8] Although such a sympathetic portrayal would become more common in the West in the latter half of the nineteenth century,[9] in the eighteenth century it was, as Boulainvilliers' anonymous English translator admitted, "new and surprizing, . . . and even contrary to all that we have hitherto been taught concerning [Muhammad]."[10]

Certainly John Wesley (1703-1791) found it so when he read the work in November of 1767. The novelty of Boulainvilliers' life of the prophet of Islam led Wesley to suspect he was reading, not history, but a "romance,"

---

4. Prideaux, *True Nature*, ii.

5. Prideaux, *True Nature*, xvi-xix. The subtitle of this work, which announces an appendix, is noteworthy in this regard: *With A Discourse annexed, for the Vindicating of Christianity from this Charge; Offered to the Consideration of the Deists of the present Age.*

6. Almond, "Western Images of Islam, 1700-1900," 413.

7. Boulainvilliers, *Life of Mahomet*, 169. The French original of this book had been published the preceding year. For a brief note on Boulainvilliers, see "Boulainvilliers, Henri," in *The Encyclopædia Britannica*, 11th ed. (New York: Encyclopædia Britannica, Inc., 1910) 4:318.

8. Boulainvilliers, *Life of Mahomet*, 170; see also 224, 244.

9. See Almond, "Western Images of Islam, 1700-1900," 412-424.

10. Boulainvilliers, *Life of Mahomet*, ii.

that is, sheer fiction at best. Comparison with Prideaux's standard life only confirmed the Methodist preacher in his opinion.

> I went to Canterbury. Here I met with the Life of Mahomet, wrote, I suppose, by the Count de Boulainvilliers. Whoever the author is, he is a very pert, shallow, self-conceited coxcomb, remarkable for nothing but his immense assurance and thorough contempt of Christianity. And the book is a dull, ill-digested romance, supported by no authorities at all; whereas Dean Prideaux (a writer of ten times his sense) cites his authorities for everything he advances.[11]

FOR THE MAHOMETANS

Implicit agreement with Prideaux's portrayal of Muhammad is also found in a little-known hymn by Charles Wesley (1707–1788) which well reveals the hymnwriter's marvelous ability to convert rich Christian doctrine into hymnody and prayer. Entitled "For the Mahometans," it employed fundamental truths of Christian orthodoxy to impart to the singer a prayerful response to what is termed "the dire apostasy" of Islam. It contains a particularly compelling example of one way in which Christians have responded to Muslims in the centuries-old encounter between their two religions, even though certain phrases of the hymn do not fall within the bounds of current political correctness or cultural knowledge.

The original appearance of this hymn was in Charles Wesley's volume *Hymns of Intercession for all Mankind* (1758). Taken out of context, it would be easy to see in the hymn an apologetic purpose with the goal of refuting Islam. However, the textual context in which the hymn was first published speaks of a somewhat different aim in Wesley's mind, namely, prayer desirous of the salvation of Muhammad's followers. His brother John also understood the hymn in this light, for he included it, along with four others from the 1758 hymnal, in a sub-section entitled "For Believers Interceding for the World" in what became the standard Methodist hymnal, *A Collection of Hymns for the Use of the People called Methodists* (1780).[12] Alongside this hymn for Muslims in the latter hymnal, there are also hymns "For the Heathens" and "For the Jews"—three categories of people mentioned in one

---

11. Journal entry for 23 November 1767, in Baker et al., *Works of John Wesley*, 22:113–114.

12. This hymnal was the product of much careful thought and arranging by John Wesley. See "Introduction: 2. The Development of the *Collection*," in Baker et al., *Works of John Wesley*, 7:22–30.

of the Collects for Good Friday from the Anglican *Book of Common Prayer*, which the Wesleys would have known well, and of which Charles was particularly fond:

> O merciful God, who hast made all men, and hatest nothing that thou hast made, nor wouldest the death of a sinner, but rather that he should be converted and live; have mercy upon all Jews, Turks, Infidels, and Hereticks, and take from them all ignorance, hardness of heart, and contempt of thy word; and so fetch them home, blessed Lord, to thy flock, that they may be saved among the remnant of the true Israelites, and be made one fold under one Shepherd, Jesus Christ our Lord, who liveth and reigneth with thee and the Holy Spirit, one God, world without end.[13]

This clear textual link to *The Book of Common Prayer* is further confirmation that the hymn "For the Mahometans" is first and foremost concerned with prayer for the salvation of Muslims.

STANZA 1: SUN OF UNCLOUDED RIGHTEOUSNESS

> Sun of unclouded righteousness,
>   With healing in thy wings arise,
> A sad benighted world to bless,
>   Which now in sin and error lies,
> Wrapt in Egyptian night profound,
> With chains of hellish darkness bound.

The hymn begins with a reference to Malachi 4:2 and its promise of the advent of the Messiah, the "Sun of righteousness," who will bring blessing to a world enchained in the "hellish darkness" of sin and doctrinal error. The Old Testament image from Malachi 4 was a favourite one with Wesley.[14] In one of his earliest hymns, which was written for the first anniversary of his conversion, and which has been transmitted as "O for a thousand tongues to sing," the second stanza of what was originally eighteen ran thus:

---

13. "Good Friday: The Collects," in *The Book of Common Prayer* (1661). For this reference to *The Book of Common Prayer* I am indebted to Watson, *English Hymn*, 220. For Charles's love of the Anglican prayer-book, see Tyson, *Charles Wesley: A Reader*, 33–34; Watson, *English Hymn*, 233–243.

14. For the various hymns containing references to Malachi 4:2, see *Works of John Wesley*, 7:819; Lawson, *Thousand Tongues*, 214; Kimbrough and Beckerlegge, *Unpublished Poetry*, 3:228, 276. See also "Jesus, my strength and righteousness," no. XVII, stanza 9, in *Hymns for Those that Seek* (1747); "Christ, whose glory fills the skies," stanza 1, *Hymns and Sacred Poems* (1740).

> On this glad day the glorious Sun
>> Of Righteousness arose,
> On my benighted soul He shone,
>> And fill'd it with repose.[15]

The phrase "Sun of Righteousness" naturally brings to mind the contrast of light and darkness. Here the hymnwriter's own "benighted soul" has been illuminated. In "For the Mahometans," the hymnwriter and singer look forward to a similar work being done in a "sad benighted world," by which is clearly meant the Muslim nations, one of them, Egypt, being specifically mentioned.

The vivid image of being "wrapped in Egyptian night profound" recalls how one of the ten plagues, the plague of "thick darkness" mentioned in Exodus 10:21–22, came "over the land of Egypt." According to the KJV rendering of the Exodus passage, it was a palpable darkness—it could be felt. In the hymn, the term "wrapped" captures the horror of being utterly surrounded by darkness. By contrast, the One who brings healing and blessing is "unclouded," without a particle of darkness.

STANZA 2: THAT IMPOSTER

> The smoke of the infernal cave,
>> Which half the Christian world o'erspread,
> Disperse, thou heavenly Light, and save
>> The souls by that Imposter led,
> That Arab thief, as Satan bold,
> Who quite destroy'd thine[16] Asian fold.

In his life of Muhammad, Prideaux had indicated Muhammad "used to withdraw himself into a solitary cave near Mecca" where, according to Prideaux's rendering, he concocted his religious beliefs,[17] an assertion reflected here in the first line of the second stanza. Picking up the theme of darkness from the first stanza, Wesley likened Muhammad's teaching to "smoke," which, spreading out from that cave near Mecca, went on to engulf half of the Christian world of that era. From the Arabian peninsula, Islam had devastated the Byzantine Empire with seemingly invincible military might. Within eighty years of the death of Muhammad, key centres of Ancient Christianity had fallen before the onslaught of Islam: Damascus

---

15. For this stanza and the other seventeen stanzas, see "For the Anniversary Day of One's Conversion" in *Hymns and Sacred Poems* (1740) 120–123; see also Chapter 3 in this volume by Jonathan Powers.

16. thy : *Collection* (1780).

17. Prideaux, *True Nature*, 14.

was conquered in 635, Jerusalem fell in 638, Alexandria was taken in 642, Carthage in 698, and by 708 the entirety of what once had been Christian North Africa was in the hands of Muslim rulers. And so, Wesley noted, Muhammad's beliefs "quite destroy'd [Christ's] Asian fold."

Prideaux had argued how the downfall of those Western Asian churches had been due to internal decay and their turning of Christ's "Holy Religion into a Firebrand of Hell for Contention, Strife, and Violence among them."[18] The hymn makes no allusion to this perspective, though John Wesley did state around the very time his brother's hymn was written: "blind and bitter zeal, and . . . endless thirst after vain jangling and strife of words . . . have reigned for many ages in the Greek Church, and well-nigh banished true religion from among them."[19] Both John and Charles had a deep appreciation for the theological riches of Eastern Orthodoxy, but that did not blind John—and presumably not Charles—to the significant problems of the churches of that communion.[20]

Noteworthy is the way Wesley described Muhammad in this stanza. The founder of Islam is "that Imposter," the way he was frequently described by eighteenth-century occidental authors, an epithet made popular by Prideaux. He is "that Arab thief," as bold as Satan in his attacks on Christianity. John had a similar opinion of the devastation caused by Muhammad and his followers. Ten years before his reading of Boulainvilliers' biography of Muhammad, the elder Wesley had stated that prior to the Deists of his day no opponent of the Christian faith had hurt Christianity as much as Muhammad.[21] As for the latter's followers, Wesley was blunt: they have "no knowledge or love of God." It should not be surprising then to find how their history had been so bloody, for, Wesley averred,

> ever since the religion of Mahomet appeared in the world, the espousers of it, . . . have been as wolves and tigers to all other nations, rending and tearing all that fell into their merciless paws, and grinding them with their iron teeth; . . . many countries, which were once as the garden of God, are now a desolate wilderness . . .[22]

---

18. Prideaux, *True Nature*, viii.

19. *The Doctrine of Original Sin, according to Scripture, Reason, and Experience* (1757), in Jackson, *Works of John Wesley*, 9:217.

20. Tore Meistad has argued the Wesleys' "soteriology and cosmology reveal that their deepest roots" are in the soil of Eastern Orthodoxy rather than the Latin Fathers. See Meistad, "The Missiology of Charles Wesley and Its Links to the Eastern Church," 205–31. See also Campbell, *John Wesley and Christian Antiquity*.

21. Letter to Augustus Montague Toplady, 9 December 1758, in Telford, *Letters of John Wesley*, 4:48.

22. *Doctrine of Original Sin* (1757) in Jackson, *Works of John Wesley*, 9:216. It needs

Nevertheless, despite this past history and the way Muslims had wrought such destruction upon the Eastern churches, Charles Wesley can pray for Christ, the "heavenly Light," to dispel their darkness and save their souls.

STANZA 3: FOR THOSE WHO SPURN THE SPRINKLED BLOOD

> O might the blood of sprinkling cry
> For those who spurn the sprinkled blood!
> Assert thy glorious Deity,
> Stretch out thine arm, thou triune God,
> The Unitarian fiend expel,
> And chase his doctrine back to hell.

Jesus Christ is mentioned in the Qur'ān some twenty-five times, where he is honoured as One who was virgin-born, a prophet, and miracle worker. But the Qur'ān explicitly rejects his crucifixion, and by extension, his resurrection.[23] It would be for this reason, among others, that John Wesley, who was quite conversant with the Qur'ān, rejected it as divine revelation. In his words, the book contained "the most gross and impious absurdities."[24] How much of the Muslim holy book Charles had read is not known, but as this third stanza makes clear he is very aware of the Muslim denial of the crucifixion. The Muslims, for whose salvation he is praying, are "those who spurn the sprinkled blood."

As John Tyson has observed, the "most common word in Charles Wesley's redemption hymns is blood."[25] Its biblical associations with death and sacrifice make it well suited to express the heart of Wesley's soteriology: the salvation of sinners is rooted in Christ's shedding of his blood on the cross,[26] his dying in the stead of all of humanity. More specifically, Tyson has shown how Wesley's use of the phrase "sprinkled blood," which is dependent in large measure on verses from the Book of Hebrews, sought to communicate

---

to be noted how on occasion John Wesley can view Islam in a more positive light. See Richie, "John Wesley and Mohammed," 79–99.

23. Qur'ān 4.157–8. Yet, there are two other texts, Qur'ān 3.54–5 and 19.27–34, which imply Christ's death. For further discussion of the Christology of the Qur'ān, see Cotterell, "The Christology of Islam," 290–95; and Parrinder, *Jesus in the Qur'ān*.

24. *Doctrine of Original Sin* (1757) in Jackson, *Works of John Wesley*, 9:216.

25. Tyson, *Charles Wesley on Sanctification*, 115. See Tyson's whole discussion of Wesley's various uses of the term "blood," 115–55.

26. His "Passion alone / Hath purchas'd our Peace," Hymn XIX, stanza 2, in *Gloria Patri, etc. Or Hymns to the Trinity* (1746) 9.

the idea of spiritual cleansing and reconciliation to God.[27] So, for example, using this image to stress the idea of reconciliation, Wesley could write:

> Jehovah's co-eternal Son
> > Did in our flesh appear beneath,
> He laid his life a ransom down,
> > For every man he tasted death,
> To justify us by His blood,
> And bring the sprinkled world to God.[28]

Similarly, in a poem based on Mark 15:34 ("My God, my God, why hast thou forsaken me!"), Wesley declared:

> Casting a dying look
> > Thy God thou cou'dst not find,
> Because thy Spirit had forsook
> > Our whole apostate kind,
> Nor could our fallen race
> > Rise and return to God,
> Or e'er retrieve thy Spirit's grace,
> > But thro' thy sprinkled blood.[29]

Thus, in using this imagery in "For the Mahometans," Wesley was praying—despite the Muslims' rejection of the crucified Christ—for his atoning work, "the blood of sprinkling," to prove efficacious and save some of them. But this will only happen, Wesley went on to assert, if God acts with divine power:

> Assert thy glorious Deity,
> Stretch out thine arm, thou triune God!

Here Wesley purposely touched on another fundamental difference between Christianity and Islam: the nature of God. In one of the central themes of the Qur'ān, "God is only one God, He is far above having a son."[30] Hence, readers of the Qur'ān are admonished: "believe in God and His messengers and do not speak of 'a Trinity.'"[31] But, Trinitarianism is central to Christianity, a fact Wesley celebrated again and again in his hymnody, for in the words of John

---

27. Tyson, *Charles Wesley on Sanctification*, 123–7.

28. Hymn DXVII (based on Romans 1:16), "Superior to all fear and shame," stanza 3, in *Short Hymns on Select Passages of the Holy Scriptures* 2 (1762).

29. Kimbrough and Beckerlegge, *Unpublished Poetry of Charles Wesley*, 2:69.

30. Qur'ān 4.171, trans. M.A.S. Abdel Haleem, in *The Qur'ān* (Oxford: University Press, 2004) 66. All further quotations of the Qur'ān are from this translation.

31. Qur'ān 4.171. See also Qur'ān 5.72–3 and 5.116–7. The latter includes Mary in the Trinity.

Tyson, the "doctrine of the Trinity pervaded Charles Wesley's theology."[32] Wesley thus encouraged those who sang his hymns to worship the

> Coequal, Coeternal Three,
> Thy Glorious Triune Deity
>   Let all Eternally proclaim.[33]

Though in this world the triunity of God far exceeded humanity's ability to explain—"Inexplicably Three and One," as Wesley said[34]—yet the Methodist hymn-writer delighted in orthodox Trinitarian declarations such as:

> Thou are the co-eternal Son,
> In substance with thy Father one,
> In person differing, we proclaim,
> In power and majesty the same.[35]

Or this:

> Three uncompounded Persons One,
>   One undivided God we proclaim:
> In essence, nature, substance one,
>   Through all eternity the same.[36]

Moreover, he was confident that in the world to come,

> There, there we shall see
>   The Substance Divine,
> And fashion'd like Thee
>   Transcendantly shine,
> Thy Personal Essence
>   Be bold to explain,

---

32. Tyson, *Charles Wesley: A Reader*, 47. For a fuller study, see Allchin, "The Trinity in the Teaching of Charles Wesley," 69–84.

33. Hymn XVIII, "Father of all above, below," stanza 2, in *Gloria Patri* (1746) 9.

34. Hymn XV, "Glory to God the Father give," in *Gloria Patri* (1746) 8; Hymn CCLII, "Holy, holy, holy Lord," stanza 3, "One inexplicably Three / One in simplest Unity," in *A Collection of Hymns* (1780); Hymn CCLV, "Thee, Father, Son, and Holy Ghost," stanza 1, in *A Collection of Hymns* (1780).

35. Hymn CCXLV, "Jesus, thou art the mighty God," stanza 2, in *A Collection of Hymns* (1780).

36. Hymn CCLV, "Thee, Father, Son, and Holy Ghost," stanza 1, in *A Collection of Hymns* (1780). See also Hymn CCXLVIII, "Hail, Father, Son, and Spirit great," stanza 2, in *A Collection of Hymns* (1780):
A mystical plurality
We in the Godhead own,
Adoring One in Persons Three,
And Three in nature One.

> And wrapt in thy Presence
>   Eternally reign.[37]

Wesley's commitment to the Trinity was also rooted in his consciousness of redemption as a Trinitarian affair:

> Come, Father, Son, and Holy Ghost,
>   Whom one all-perfect God we own,
> Restorer of thine image lost,
>   Thy various offices make known;
> Display, our fallen souls to raise,
> Thy whole economy of grace.
>
> Jehovah in Three Persons, come,
>   And draw, and sprinkle us, and seal . . .[38]

Little wonder then how Wesley regarded the denial of the Trinity, which robbed God of his glory and undermined the economy of redemption, as a "doctrine . . . [from] hell."

One final point about this third stanza, which needs to be noted, ties it to the larger historical context in which the hymn was written. By terming Islamic theology "Unitarian," Wesley was linking it to one of the major theological challenges of his day, namely the rise and expansion of Socinianism or Unitarianism among both Anglicans and Dissenters. In fact, around the same time when Charles would have been writing this hymn or even preparing it for publication, his brother was engaged in writing one of his major works, *The Doctrine of Original Sin* (1757), a detailed response to John Taylor (1694–1761), pastor of the Presbyterian work in Norwich, in that day one of the leading towns in England.[39] A well-known Hebraist, Taylor also became infamous for being, as his latest biographer G.T. Eddy has put it, a "radical champion of freedom of thought on theological questions."[40] In particular, Taylor's *The Scripture Doctrine of Original Sin* (1740) was viewed as a powerful attack on confessional Christianity on both sides of the Atlantic.[41] Proof of this is found among those who published a response to it, including John Wesley, and most notably Jonathan Edwards

---

37. Hymn XIX, "Thee Father of men," stanza 4, *Gloria Patri* (1746) 10. For a similar thought, see Hymn CCCXXIV, "Come on, my partners in distress," stanzas 5–6, *A Collection of Hymns* (1780).

38. Hymn CCLIII, stanzas 1–2, in *A Collection of Hymns* (1780).

39. For a critical overview and analysis of Wesley's work, see Schmidt, *John Wesley: A Theological Biography*, 2/2:80–97.

40. Eddy, *Dr. Taylor of Norwich*, 40.

41. Baker et al., *Works of John Wesley*, 20:245–6, n. 47.

(1703–1758), the most important American theologian of the eighteenth century. Imbued with the optimistic confidence in human reason typical of so many in his day, Taylor also deprecated what he called "Athanasianism," which is Nicene Trinitarianism, because of what he believed to be its denial of God's unity.[42] Eddy thinks Taylor was probably closest to Arianism in his theological convictions,[43] but John Wesley thought otherwise and regarded Taylor as a Unitarian.

When Charles refers to Muhammad as a "Unitarian fiend" then, he is making vivid for his contemporaries the deep concern Christians ought to have about the theological perspectives of Islam. It is noteworthy how John Wesley could tell fellow hymnwriter Augustus Montague Toplady (1740–1778) in December of 1758—the year in which Charles Wesley published "For the Mahometans"—that "no single person since Mahomet has given such a wound to Christianity as Dr. Taylor."[44]

STANZA 4: LORD OF THE CREATION REIGN

> Come, Father, Son and Holy Ghost,
>   Thou Three in One, and One in Three!
> Resume thine[45] own, for ages lost,
>   Finish the dire apostasy;
> Thy universal claim maintain,
> And Lord of the creation reign!

Over against Islam's Unitarianism, Wesley's Christian faith, as we have seen, affirms a Triunity within the Godhead. Wesley now calls on this Triune Being to bring an end to the rule of Islam. He has one parting remark about the religion founded by Muhammad: it is a "dire apostasy." This interpretation views Islam as an heretical departure from Christianity, a perspective stretching back to one of the earliest Christian respondents to Islam, the theologian John of Damascus (ca. 655/675–ca. 749), who included it in his *On Heresies*.[46]

---

42. Eddy, *Dr. Taylor of Norwich*, 40.

43. Eddy, *Dr. Taylor of Norwich*, 40, 150–2.

44. Letter to Augustus Montague Toplady, 9 December 1758, in Telford, *Letters of John Wesley*, 4:48.

45. thy : *Collection* (1780).

46. For the section of this work dealing with Islam, see Chase, *Saint John of Damascus*. 37:153–160. See also Sahas, *John of Damascus on Islam*. For a general study of the life and thought of John of Damascus, see Louth, *St. John Damascene*.

The hymn ends, though, on a positive stress on the universality of the Christian Faith: the Triune God is the Creator of everything in existence and thus has a right to reign as creation's Lord. This includes all of humanity, and thus, in the context of this hymn, there is here an implicit challenge for missions to the Muslims.[47]

Rightly understood, this hymn is a prayer for the salvation of the Muslims, but it ends with an implicit call to action—namely missionary outreach to the Muslim nations. In this respect it is similar to another hymn included in the same volume of hymns. This one was entitled "For the Heathens":[48]

> Lord over all, if thou hast made,
>   Hast ransom'd every soul of man,
> Why is the grace so long delay'd,
>   Why unfulfill'd the saving plan?
> The bliss for Adam's race design'd,
> When will it reach to all mankind?
>
> Art thou the God of the Jews alone,
>   And not the God of Gentiles too?
> To Gentiles make thy goodness known,
>   Thy judgment to the nations show;
> Awaken them by the gospel call;
> Light of the world, illumine all.[49]

---

47. Tore Meistad has noted, "Most of Charles Wesley's hymns included implicit challenges for missions." See Meistad, "The Missiology of Charles Wesley: An Introduction," 39.

48. Hymn XXXIV, stanzas 1–2, in *Hymns of Intercession for All Mankind* (1758).

49. A version of this paper was previously published as "'For Those who Spurn the Sprinkled Blood!' Praying with Charles Wesley for Muslims," in *Southwestern Journal of Theology* 49/2 (Spring 2007) 186–98.

Hymn Tunes & Hymnals

13

Operatic influences on the hymn tunes used by John and Charles Wesley

MARGARET GARRETT

John Wesley (1703–1791) and his brother Charles (1707–1788) might have agreed on most theological issues, but the brothers had very different ideas about music. John, who was not a musician, was very conservative in his musical tastes. Charles, however, had two sons training to be professional musicians. Due to this, he was more open-minded about music both inside and outside the church. Charles enjoyed the Italian opera popular during his time and parodied some of its arias into hymns by Christianizing the texts. Charles and John both were acquainted with some of London's finest contemporary opera composers, such as George Frideric Handel, Thomas Augustine Arne, and John Frederick Lampe. Baroque opera put an indelible mark on hymn tunes used by John and Charles Wesley and their Methodist Societies. This study will explore how Baroque opera influenced those hymn tunes by discussing the musical philosophies of the Wesley brothers, the composers who wrote Methodist hymns, and the relevant published hymnals of that era.

JOHN WESLEY'S MUSICAL PHILOSOPHY

John Wesley had definite ideas about what he considered to be good music for religious services. He wrote "Directions for Singing" (1761),[1] as well as

1. Part of *Select Hymns with Tunes Annext* (1761).

an essay entitled "Thoughts on the Power of Music" (1781).[2] An advocate of the Renaissance form of monody, or solo singing on one melody, as the music best suited for congregational singing, he felt "modern music has less power than the ancient."[3] It was his opinion that counterpoint diminished the comprehensibility of the text, leaving part-singing and figured bass to be excessive ornaments. John believed the sole purpose for music in the church was to spread the message of the sacred text. Wesleyan scholar Steven Darsey wrote, "Wesley was inconsistent in the application of his musical philosophy. He did not believe in harmony on the one hand, yet he published his 1780 *Sacred Harmony* in two and three parts. He condemned counterpoint, yet granted its devotional efficacy in notable instances."[4] However, counterpoint was not as much of an issue for him outside of the church. He was said to have attended and apparently enjoyed George Frideric Handel's oratorios, the choruses of which were laden with examples of finely woven counterpoint.

Another prominent Wesleyan scholar, Carlton R. Young, discussed the Wesley brothers' relationship with music in his book *Music of the Heart*. According to Young, "Methodism's tune repertory was greatly expanded in John Wesley's collections to include those composed or adapted to accommodate the increasing number of meters in Charles Wesley's hymns: folk tunes; vocal and instrumental melodies from Italian opera and Handelian sacred and secular oratorio; and highly ornamented melody scored in basso-continuo solo social style and accompanied by a viol or string bass, organ, or harpsichord."[5] Opera, oratorio, the broadsheet ballad, the parlor song, and folk music were the types of music popular with the Wesleys' educated constituents.[6] Although John Wesley did not accept all forms of popular music, he did use opera and oratorio excerpts in *A Collection of Tunes . . . Sung at the Foundery* (1742), in *Select Hymns with Tunes Annext* (1761), and in *Sacred Harmony* (1780).

CHARLES WESLEY'S MUSICAL PHILOSOPHY

Charles Wesley was more open-minded about the music prevalent in the concert halls and churches of London than was his brother. He enjoyed both

---

2. Dated 9 June 1779 in *Arminian Magazine* 4 (1781) 103–7; also in Baker et al., *Works of John Wesley*, 7:766–9.

3. Young, *Music of the Heart*, 90.

4. Darsey, "John Wesley as Hymn and Tune Editor," 22.

5. Young, *Music of the Heart*, 103–4.

6. Young, *Music of the Heart*, 104.

the vocal and instrumental music of his day. His two sons were talented musicians and performed concerts of their own music occasionally. Charles so admired music that he wrote poems about it and about those who perform it. In his poem, "Modern Music," he expressed his thoughts on the Italian and German music of the day.

> *Modern Music*
> G —, B —,[7] and all
> Their followers, great and small,
> Have cut Old Music's throat,
> And mangled every note;
> Their superficial pains
> Have dashed out all his brains:
> And now we dote upon
> A lifeless sceleton,
> The empty sound at most,
> The Squeak of Music's ghost.[8]

He wrote a poem about "The Pianoforte" in 1783.[9] His poem "Written in Kelway's Sonatas" is a criticism of the British composer Joseph Kelway (1702–1782).[10] In addition, he wrote a poem defending classical music to its critics in the church and one about his own lack of formal musical training.

A great admirer of talented performers, Charles wrote the hymn "To Miss Davis" as a tribute to Cecelia Davies (ca. 1756–1836), a popular vocalist from England who was the first Englishwoman to appear on the Italian stage. Called *L'Inglesina* by her Italian fans, she was considered to be an expert in performing Italian opera.

> *To Miss Davis*
> Gentle Inglesina, say
> Can the smooth Italian Lay
> Nature's ruggedness remove,
> Soften Britons into love?
> Yes; the stocks & stones draw near,
> Thy inchanting Voice to hear
> And all the Savages agree
> In praise of harmony & Thee![11]

---

7. Probably Felice de Giardini and Johann Christian Bach.
8. Kimbrough and Beckerlegge, *Unpublished Poetry*, 3:383.
9. Kimbrough and Beckerlegge, *Unpublished Poetry*, 3:385.
10. Kimbrough and Beckerlegge, *Unpublished Poetry*, 3:382–3.
11. Kimbrough and Beckerlegge, *Unpublished Poetry*, 3:380.

Charles wrote two poems to honor George Frideric Handel.[12] Handel was also mentioned in the homage Charles wrote to commemorate the death of composer William Boyce (1711–1779).[13]

WHAT'S IN A NAME?

Several of the tunes cited in this study have multiple names, such as Lampe's INVITATION, which is also called BANBURY, DEVONSHIRE, KENT, and WILTON. Name variations such as these were common among eighteenth-century hymn tunes, as hymn tune book compilers renamed tunes unpredictably. This makes researching the genealogy of hymn tunes from the era extremely difficult. The tunes must be confirmed by counting musical intervals, not by tracing names.[14] Methodist hymnbook editor Thomas Butts (fl. 1760) took several liberties with hymn tune names when he published his editions of *Harmonia Sacra* in 1753, 1756, 1763, and 1816 (in America). Methodists used the 1756 edition widely during the eighteenth century. Many of its tunes were adapted from instrumental and theater sources. Nine were from Handel's operas and oratorios, two were from Thomas Arne's operas, and two were from Lampe's *Ladies Amusement* (1749). Also included were 22 of Lampe's theater-song style tunes from his collection of hymn tunes written for Charles Wesley's poetry, *Hymns on the Great Festivals and Other Occasions* (1746).

Apparently, John Wesley tolerated the societies' use of these tunes until he published *Select Hymns with Tunes Annext* (1761), in which he followed Butts' example by incorporating a number of theater melodies, including a tune from Henry Purcell's (1659–1695) opera *King Arthur*.

HENRY PURCELL

Henry Purcell (1659–1695) is known as one of the greatest English composers of all time. He wrote vocal and instrumental music, including operas, church anthems, odes, fantasias, suites, and voluntaries. In his opera *King Arthur*, using lyrics by John Dryden, Venus sings the aria "Fairest isle, all isles excelling" in the last act (Figure 1). Charles Wesley's hymn "Love divine, all loves excelling" was apparently intended to be sung to Purcell's

---

12. Kimbrough and Beckerlegge, *Unpublished Poetry*, 3:381–2.

13. "Ode on the death of Dr. Boyce," broadsheet (1779); Handel was named twice, in sts. 2–3.

14. Stevenson, "The Eighteenth-Century Hymn Tune," 8.

tune. The hymn's structure, phraseology, and language all reflect Dryden's poem (Figure 2). In essence, Charles Wesley turned words sung by the goddess of love into words to be sung to the God of love. It is the best known of his hymns written in imitatation of earlier poems or written to make use of popular tunes. In *Divine Music Miscellany* (1754), a tunebook intended for George Whitefield's congregation, the tune was called DUBLIN and was paired with "Loving Saviour, Prince of peace," but the tune was more commonly known as WESTMINSTER, including in the Wesleys' tunebooks.[15] In the 1780 *Collection of Hymns*,[16] this tune had also been recommended for use with "Righteous God, whose vengeful phials" (no. 59), "Light of life, seraphic fire" (no. 387), and "Come, thou all-inspiring Spirit" (no. 516). Purcell's tune WESTMINSTER is very rarely included in present-day hymnals.

Fig. 1. Henry Purcell, *King Arthur* (1691), lyrics by John Dryden.

15. For more on this tune's publication history, and other tunes named in this study, see Temperley, *Hymn Tune Index*.

16. In this collection, tune designations were included in the 5th, 6th, and 7th eds. (1786, 1788, 1791).

Love divine, all loves excelling

Fig. 2. WESTMINSTER, *Select Hymns with Tunes Annext* (1761), text by Charles Wesley.

If one looks at the above examples and compares Purcell's "Fairest isle, all isles excelling" with "Love divine, all loves excelling" (WESTMINSTER), one can see how the two tunes have the same melodic structure and the same length, although in many places the hymn tune has added some passing tones, or in other places removed or lessened them. In the hymn tune, the rhythmic values have been doubled, and the key has been transposed down a minor third. In spite of the alterations, one is still clearly derivative of the other.

Other hymn tunes written by Purcell include COLCHESTER and WESTMINSTER ABBEY. Another tune, WALSALL (not to be confused with the tune by Lampe and used by the Wesleys), is sometimes attributed to Purcell, but it was not published until the 1720s. BURFORD is also doubtfully attributed to Purcell.

THOMAS AUGUSTINE ARNE

Thomas Augustine Arne (1710–1778) was a British composer who was a contemporary of the Wesleys, Handel, and Lampe. He is known to have published several of Lampe's works following Lampe's death. Feeling overshadowed by Handel, he shied away from writing oratorio until after Handel's death. However, he is known for his contributions to vocal music, in particular, Italian-style English operas. The hymn tune ARNE is an arrangement of the aria "Waters parted from the sea," from his opera *Artaxerxes* (1762). Its first appearance as a hymn tune was in Thomas Knibb's *Psalm Singer's Help* (ca. 1769). It was included in John Wesley's *Sacred Harmony* (1780). In the 1780 *Collection*, ARNE was associated with two hymns: "Happy soul, that free from harms" (no. 13) and "What are these arrayed in white" (no. 74). ARLINGTON also has roots in *Atexerxes*, from the overture.

The Wesleys used a hymn tune derived from Arne's opera *Eliza* (1754), from the air "My fond shepherds of late." This was included in the second edition of *Select Hymns* (1765), where it was called THOU SHEPHERD OF ISRAEL after Charles's hymn, "Thou Shepherd of Israel, and mine" (no. 145 in that collection). This tune has also been called AT LYING DOWN, SALTERS, and INVOCATION. The other Wesley hymns paired this tune in the 1780 *Collection* were "I long to behold him arrayed" (no. 68), "Come, holy, celestial Dove," (no. 159), "All glory to God in the sky" (no. 211), and "What now is my object and aim?" (no. 360). The tunes FALKIRK and MUSICIAN'S have also been ascribed to Arne.

JONATHAN BATTISHILL

C. Jonathan Battishill (1738–1801) worked as a conductor, singer, and church organist, and he composed theater music (including one opera), anthems, glees, and songs. He co-composed the opera *Almena* with Michael Arne (1740–1786), the illegitimate son of Thomas Arne.[17] He set twelve of Charles's hymns from *Hymns and Sacred Poems* (1749), published as a small booklet, *Twelve Hymns*, ca. 1765.[18] His tunes were highly ornamented melodies, "presumably for a trained singer, with figured bass accompaniment."[19]

---

17. John A. Parkinson, "Michael Arne," in *Grove Music Online*.
18. Battishill, *Twelve Hymns, The Words by the Rev'd Mr. Charles Wesley M.A.*
19. Young, *Music from the Heart*, 172.

HENRY CAREY

Henry Carey (ca. 1692–1743) was a musician who collaborated with Lampe in a series of operas. His namesake tune, CAREY'S (also called SURREY and CAREY'S SURREY), first appeared in John Church's *Introduction to Psalmody* (ca. 1723), set to Joseph Addison's "The Lord my pasture shall prepare." The Wesleys included it in *Select Hymns* (1761) and *Sacred Harmony* (1780). The tune was originally composed for solo voice and continuo. In the 1780 *Collection*, it was appointed for several hymns, including, "Sinners, obey the gospel word" (no. 31) and "Jesu, thy boundless love to me" (no. 362). CAREY'S was used in *The United Methodist Hymnal* (1989) with hymn 579, "Lord God, your love has called us here." The text was written by Brian Wren in 1973 as an attempt to restate Charles's "And can it be that I should gain."[20]

The tune JUDGMENT, included in the 1761 and 1780 tunebooks, is based on a song in Henry Carey's *Britannia*, which he wrote in celebration of Admiral Edward Vernon's capture of Portobelo, Panama, in 1739. Similar to "Love divine, all loves excelling," Charles Wesley parodied the original text, turning "He comes! he comes! the hero comes!" into "He comes! he comes! the Judge severe," a hymn about Christ's second coming.[21] The tune was also commonly called TRUMPET. SALISBURY, the tune associated with "Christ the Lord is ris'n today," has sometimes been ascribed to Henry Carey, although its true authorship is uncertain.

JOHN FREDERICK LAMPE

Carey's opera collaborator, John Frederick Lampe (1703–1751), has been called "the first Methodist composer."[22] The Wesleys probably came to know Lampe through Mrs. Priscilla Stevens Rich, an actress at Covent Garden who was also a convert to Methodism. In 1744, she married Covent Garden owner John Rich, who converted to Methodism later in their marriage. Much to her husband's dismay, she denounced her occupation as an actress after her conversion. As an influential member of London society, she apparently introduced the Wesleys to Lampe and several other prominent musicians, including Handel. In November of 1745, Lampe came under the

---

20. Sanchez, *Hymns of the Methodist Hymnal*, 197.

21. Charles's hymn text was first published in *Hymns of Intercession for all Mankind* (1758), repeated in *Select Hymns* (1761), *Collection of Hymns* (1780), and *Pocket Hymn Book*, 2nd ed. (1787).

22. Lightwood, *Methodist Music*, title of chapter 4.

influence of the Wesleys and converted to Methodism after speaking with John Wesley. On November 29, 1745, John Wesley wrote in his journal, "I spent an hour with Mr. Lampe, who had been a Deist for many years, till it pleased God, by the *Earnest Appeal [to Men of Reason and Religion*, 1743] to bring him to a better mind."[23] Shortly thereafter, he began composing hymn tunes for use in the Methodist Society meetings.

Originally from Saxony, Germany, Lampe settled in England around 1725 and played bassoon in Handel's opera and oratorio orchestra. He was known as a performer, teacher, and theoretician. As a composer, he focused on writing satires and burlesques for the theater. His most successful work was the comedic operetta, *The Dragon of Wantley* (1738). Some of his mature operas include *Margery, Pyramus and Thisbe, Dione*, and *Amelia*. In addition to composing, he wrote two treatises on music theory, *A Plain and Compendious Method of Teaching Thorough Bass* (1737) and *The Art of Musick* (1740).

As a hymn tune composer, he is best known for his collection of twenty-four tunes set to Charles Wesley's texts, *Hymns on the Great Festivals and Other Occasions* (1746). This was the first group of original tunes written specifically for Methodist hymns. It is suspected Lampe paid for the publication himself.[24]

Lampe's writing is known to be "Italianate and florid."[25] His tunes were apparently written for presentation by soloists or by a group of trained singers. He might have written them for his wife to sing. Lampe's wife, Isabella, was one of the leading operatic sopranos of her day. She also happened to be sister-in-law of composer Thomas Arne.[26] The figured bass in his hymn tune settings indicates they were to be accompanied by harpsichord and cello, as opposed to hymns in the *Foundery* collection (1742), which were melody-only. They could have been intended for performance for affluent audiences, including theater musicians and patrons with whom Charles would have associated while he promoted his sons' musical careers.[27] In some churches, his hymns were performed by solo voices in their original settings, but in others, they were sung in the congregational style found in Butts' *Harmonia Sacra* (1753) and Wesley's *Select Hymns* (1761). In *Select Hymns*, Lampe's florid tunes were modified, printing them without their

23. Curnock, *Journal of John Wesley*, 3:226.

24. Martin, *Operas and Operatic Style*, 72; see also the facsimile edition of *Hymns on the Great Festivals* published by the Charles Wesley Society (1996) with commentary by Carlton R. Young, Frank Baker, Robin A. Leaver, and S.T. Kimbrough Jr.

25. Martin, *Operas and Operatic Style*, 91.

26. Peter Holman, "John Frederick Lampe," in *Grove Music Online*.

27. Young, *Music of the Heart*, 109.

original figured bass, so they would be more suitable for congregational singing. In *Sacred Harmony* (1780), they were harmonized "In two or three parts for the voice, harpsichord & organ," but the figured bass was not restored.[28]

Thomas Butts thought so much of Lampe's writing, he included two songs from Lampe's *Ladies Amusement* in addition to 22 of his theater-style tunes from *Hymns on the Great Festivals and Other Occasions* in his *Harmonia Sacra* (1756).

Charles and John encouraged Methodist societies to use Lampe's tunes in their meetings. Regarding Lampe, Charles wrote to his friend Ebenezer Blackwell, December 11, 1746, "His tunes are universally admired here among the musical men, and have brought me into high favour with them."[29] Charles indicated for some of Lampe's tunes to be used with the texts in *Graces Before and After Meat* (1747).[30] The first twenty-four texts in *Hymns for Those That Seek and Those That Have Redemption in the Blood of Jesus Christ* (1747) were designed to be paired with the Lampe's tunes in *Hymns on the Great Festivals*. The twenty-fifth hymn, "The Musician's," is believed to have been written in honor of Lampe's conversion to Christianity.[31] Lampe went to Ireland in 1749, and then to Edinburgh to conduct and produce his works. He is sometimes credited with editing a Dublin edition of Wesley hymns, *A Collection of Hymns and Sacred Poems* (1749), which contained 22 tunes.[32] After Lampe died in 1751, Charles wrote a tribute, "On the death of Mr. Lampe," which was later published in the second series of *Funeral Hymns*.[33]

> *On the death of Mr. Lampe*
> 'Tis done! the Sovereign will's obey'd,
> The soul by angel-guards convey'd
>   Has took its seat on high;
> The brother on my choice is gone,
> To music sweeter than his own,
>   And concerts in the sky.

---

28. Young, *Music of the Heart*, 110.
29. Newport and Lloyd, *Letters of Charles Wesley*, 1:130.
30. Young, *Music of the Heart*, 109.
31. Young, *Music of the Heart*, 178–80.
32. Martin, *Operas and Operatic Style*, 76. For the tunes in the 1749 ed., see Temperley's *Hymn Tune Index*, source #CHSP; John Wesley had edited a different Dublin edition two years earlier, *Hymns and Sacred Poems* (1747); see Maddox, *John Wesley's Poetry, Hymn, and Verse*.
33. *Funeral Hymns* [Second Series] (1759), no. 16.

His spirit mounting on the wing,
Rejoic'd to hear the convoy sing,
    While harping at his side:
With ease he caught their heav'nly strain,
And smil'd, and sung in mortal pain;
    He sung, and smil'd and died.

Enroll'd with that harmonious throng,
He hears th' unutterable song,
    Th' unutterable name;
He sees the matter of the choir,
He bows, and strikes the golden lyre,
    And hymns the glorious Lamb.

He hymns the glorious Lamb alone;
No more constrain'd to make his moan
    In this sad wilderness,
To toil for sublunary pay,
And cast his sacred strains away,
    And stoop the world to please.

Redeem'd from earth, the tuneful soul,
While everlasting ages roll,
    His triumph shall prolong;
His noblest faculties exert,
And all the music of his heart
    Shall warble on his tongue.

O that my mournful days were past,
O that I might o'ertake at last
    My happy friend above;
With him the Church triumphant join
And celebrate in strains divine
    The majesty of love!

Great God of love, prepare my heart,
And tune it now to bear a part
    In heav'nly melody;
"I'll strive to sing as loud as they,
Who sit enthron'd in brighter day,"
    And nearer the Most High.

O that the promis'd time were come,
O that we all were taken home,

> Our Master's joy to share!
> Draw, Lord, the living vocal stones,
> Jesus, recall thy banish'd ones,
>   To chant thy praises there.
>
> Our number and our bliss complete,
> And summon all the choir to meet
>   Thy glorious throne around,
> The whole musician-band bring in,
> And give the signal to begin,
>   And let the trumpet sound.

Lampe's hymn tunes were very popular in the Methodist congregations. The sustained use of Lampe's hymns by "Methodists and others demonstrate[s] that Methodist music and music-making in Wesley's time was more stylistically diverse than previously thought."[34] His tune INVITATION (also called BANBURY, WILTON, DEVONSHIRE, or KENT) appears in more than 200 collections, reprints, and revisions. This tune is no. 18 in *Hymns on the Great Festivals*. Its name is derived from the theme of the opening words, "Sinners, obey the gospel-word." INVITATION is one of two tunes from Lampe's 1746 collection to be included in recent hymnals, the other being DYING STEPHEN, which was intended for the hymn "Head of the church triumphant."

ASCENSION was no. 11 in Lampe's 1746 collection, where it was set to "Hail the day that sees him rise." In the 1780 *Collection*, this tune was paired with "Hark, a voice divides the sky" (no. 50), "Meet and right it is to praise" (no. 228), and "Christ, from whom all blessings flow" (no. 504).

Although the origin of BIRMINGHAM is unknown, it has Lampe's florid style. This tune has also been called STAFFORD and SOMERTON.[35] In *Select Hymns* (1761), it was paired with "Thou hidden source of calm repose." In the 1780 *Collection*, it was recommended for that hymn (no. 201), plus "And can it be, that I should gain" (no. 193).

CALVARY is no. 5 of Lampe's *Hymns on the Great Festivals,* where it was set to "Lamb of God, whose bleeding love." It has also been called CRUCIFIXION.[36] Texts for this tune in the 1780 *Collection* were "Jesu, let thy pitying eye" (no. 103), "Let the world their virtue boast" (no. 111), and "The Woman of Canaan" (no. 158).

---

34. Young, *Music of the Heart*, 110.
35. Adams, *Musical Sources for John Wesley's Tunebooks*, 166.
36 Adams, *Musical Sources for John Wesley's Tunebooks*, 396.

RESURRECTION first appeared as no. 8 in *Hymns on the Great Festivals* with "Rejoice, the Lord is King." It originally had an active figured bass throughout.

Other hymn tunes from Lampe's 1746 collection include: LAMPE'S (no. 1); NEW YEAR'S DAY (no. 3); PASSION (no. 4); MAGDALEN (no. 10); SHEFFIELD (no. 13), also called ON THE ASCENSION, used with "Infinite God, to thee we raise"; WHIT SUNDAY (no. 14), which is through-composed; TRINITY (no. 17); CHAPEL (no. 19), for "O love divine, how sweet thou art"; WALSALL (no. 21), used for "Ye servants of God, your master proclaim"; FUNERAL (no. 22), for "Ah! lovely appearance of death"; and TRIUMPH, (no. 23) set with "On the Death of a Believer," also sometimes called MARLBROUGH.

Several hymn tunes of unknown origin have been attributed to Lampe, such as DERBY, now called DERBE; FOUNDERY, entitled FOR THE EPIPHANY in *Harmonia Sacra* and *Divine Musical Miscellany*, and used in the Wesleys' *Select Hymns* and *Sacred Harmony*; HAMILTON'S, called CLARKE'S in *Harmonia Sacra* (the attribution to Lampe was suggested by Charles Wesley Jr.);[37] MUSICIAN'S, which has been credited to either Lampe or Arne; and TRUMPET, which is also called ON THE DEATH OF A BELIEVER; and WEDNESBURY.

GEORGE FRIDERIC HANDEL

As with Lampe, the Wesleys' personal acquaintance with Handel came through the influence of Mr. and Mrs. Rich. The following note by Charles's daughter, Sarah, printed in the December 1826 issue of *The Wesleyan-Methodist Magazine*, offers some context:

> Mr. Rich was the proprietor of the Covent-Garden Theatre, which he offered to Handel, to perform his Oratorios in, when he had incurred the displeasure of the Opera party. Mrs. Rich was one of the first who attended the [Methodist] West-Street Chapel [in London's West End], and was impressed with deep seriousness by the preaching of my dear Father, who became her intimate friend; upon which she gave up the stage entirely, and suffered much reproach from her husband. . . . She was afterwards a widow, and . . . when I was young, we used to visit her at Chelsea. . . . Handel taught Mr. Rich's daughters; and it was thus that my Father and Mother used to hear his fine performances.

---

37. Baker et al., *Works of John Wesley*, 7:774.

> By the intimacy of Mr. and Mrs. Rich with Handel, he was doubtless led to set to music these Hymns of my Father.[38]

The hymns mentioned here are a set of three texts by Charles set to music by Handel, not published in either of their lifetimes, but preserved in a manuscript held at the Fitzwilliam Museum. Charles wrote two tributes to Handel. The first was "Ode on Handel's Birthday." Charles's son Samuel was born on Feb. 24, giving the day an extra special meaning:

> *Ode on Handel's Birthday*
> *S. Matthias' Day, Febr. 24*
> Hail the bright auspicious Day
> That gave Immortal Handel birth.
> Let every moment glide away
> In solemn joy and sacred mirth;
> Let every soul like his aspire
> And catch a glowing spark of pure etherial fire.[39]

After Handel's death in 1759, Charles wrote the following brief tribute:

> *Written in Handel's Lessons*
> Here all the mystic Powers of sound,
> The Soul of Harmony is found,
> Its perfect Character receives,
> And Handel dead for ever lives![40]

Regarding Handel's manuscript hymn tunes, around 1747 he wrote three tunes for solo voice and figured bass, intended to be set to three of Charles Wesley's hymns. Lampe had already set all three of these hymns in *Hymns for the Great Festivals*, thus Handel was probably aware of this collection.[41] It is not known why Handel wrote these musical settings, which were not found until several years after his death. Samuel Wesley (1766–1837), son of Charles, found the manuscript at the Fitzwilliam Museum at Cambridge in 1826. He wrote realizations of Handel's bass and published them in 1826 as *The Fitzwilliam Music, Never Published, Three Hymns, the Words by the late Revd Charles Wesley, A.M . . . Set to Music by George Frederick Handel . . . faithfully transcribed . . . by Samuel Wesley, and now very respectfully presented to the Wesleyan Society at large*. A facsimile

---

38. Wilson, "Handel's Tunes," 32–34, citing *The Wesleyan-Methodist Magazine*, Third Series, 5 (Dec. 1826) 817.

39. From a MS, Dr. E.T. Clark Collection, in Baker, *Representative Verse*, 311; Baker notes Handel was born 23 Feb. 1685, baptized 24 Feb. 1865, St. Matthias' Day.

40. From MS Patriotism Misc, page 5; in Baker, *Representative Verse*, 311.

41. Wilson, "Handel and the Hymn Tune: I," 20.

of Handel's manuscript was reproduced in John Wilson's articles for the British and American hymn societies in 1985.

The first hymn in Handel's manuscript was "Sinners, obey the gospel word"; this tune is now generally called CANNONS.[42] It is in long meter (8.8.8.8) and is catalogued as HWV 284.[43] Versions of this hymn setting appear in the *Methodist Hymnal* (1876, 1889), *The English Hymnal* (1906), *Songs of Praise* (1931), *Hymns Ancient & Modern Revised* (1950), *The BBC Hymn Book* (1951), and *100 Hymns for Today* (1969).

The second hymn is "O Love divine, how sweet thou art." In Handel's manuscript, the tune was labeled "Desiring to Love," but it is usually called FITZWILLIAM, after the museum where the tunes were found. It is catalogued as HWV 285. It was included in the *Methodist Hymnal* (1876) and the *Anglican Hymnbook* (1868). This tune is best when sung by a soloist or choir. FITZWILLIAM was edited and realized by Dr. Frances Westbrook for the British Methodist *School Hymn-Book* (1950). Just as this hymn text is sung to other tunes, this tune is sung with other hymns, including "Jesus, thou soul of all our joys," as in the British *Methodist Hymn Book* (1933) and *Hymns and Psalms* (1983).

The third hymn Handel set for Charles Wesley is "Rejoice, the Lord is King." In the manuscript, this is labeled "On the Resurrection," but it is generally known as GOPSAL.[44] The tune is in the irregular meter 6.6.6.6.8.8., and it is catalogued as HWV 286. Handel included instructions in both "Desiring to Love" and "On the Resurrection" that each half of the hymn should be repeated. According to John Wilson, "This must surely refer to a performance of the first stanza alone; it would become tedious through a whole hymn."[45] The repeat could have been ornamented by a soloist or sung *tutti* if the first time through was sung by a soloist.

Of these three hymn tunes written by Handel, GOPSAL ("On the Resurrection") is the favorite of modern congregations. The exuberant and joyful meter of GOPSAL was known in early American hymnody as Hallelujah Meter.[46] Even though "Rejoice, the Lord is king" is still sung to GOPSAL in Great Britain, Americans more often sing the text to the tune DARWALL. Found in *The United Methodist Hymnal* (1989) as no. 716, Wilson said

---

42. Wilson, "Handel's Tunes," 35, said CANNONS was named in honor of "the mansion near Edgware of the Duke of Chandos whom Handel served for several years."

43. Anthony Hicks, "George Frederic Handel," in *Grove Music Online*.

44. Wilson, "Handel's Tunes," 35, said GOPSAL was named in honor of the mansion "in Leicestershire of Charles Jennens, Handel's librettist for *Messiah* and other works."

45. Wilson, "Handel and the Hymn Tune: I," 22.

46. Sanchez, *Hymns of the Methodist Hymnal*, 238–9.

GOPSAL is "our only example of a hymn tune by one of the greatest composers still sung to the English words for which it was written."[47]

HYMN TUNES BORROWED FROM HANDEL'S OPERAS

Several other hymn tunes have been made from arrangements of parts of Handel's works. Nicholas Temperley's *Hymn Tune Index* lists at least 60 Handel arrangements made prior to 1800.[48] Because rural populations rarely saw live performances, it was a delight for them to be able to sing a favorite melody from a stage show, be it at home or at church. Thus, Handel hymn tunes were popular. The growing Methodist revival also spread popularity of hymn tunes because they expressed "a strong personal evangelism in song."[49]

The soprano aria "Non vi piacque" from Handel's opera *Siroe, rè di Persia* (*Cyrus, King of Persia*, 1728) became the tune called CHRISTMAS, known in Britain as LUNENBURG. Dr. Samuel Arnold and J.W. Callcott first published the tune in *The Psalms of David for the use of Parish Churches* (1791), for Psalm 72. Dr. Arnold came across the tune as he was editing the complete works of Handel. This tune is most often used with "While shepherds watched their flocks by night" from Tate & Brady's *Supplement to the New Version* (1700).

The march from the third act of Handel's opera *Riccardo Primo* (*Richard the First*, 1727) was included in the 1742 *Foundery* collection as JERICHO TUNE, set to John's translation of Paul Gerhardt's hymn, "Commit thou all thy griefs." Hildbrandt and Beckerlegge called this "the earliest example of a popular tune being seized on by Wesley."[50] In the 1761 and 1780 tunebooks, it was renamed HANDEL'S MARCH and appropriately set to "Soldiers of Christ, arise." In the 1780 *Collection*, this tune was recommended for "But above all, lay hold" (no. 259) and "In fellowship alone" (no. 260).

Hymn tune adaptations of the instrumental music from Handel's operas also gained popularity. After John Wesley used a march from an opera, other music editors decided to set hymns to marches as well. Marches from Handel's opera *Scipio* (1726) and his oratorio *Saul* (1739) found their way into eighteenth-century tune books.

---

47. Wilson, "Handel and the Hymn Tune: I," 22.
48. Wilson, "Handel and the Hymn Tune: II," 25.
49. Wilson, "Handel and the Hymn Tune: II," 25.
50. Baker et al., *Works of John Wesley*, 7:778.

HYMN TUNES BORROWED FROM HANDEL'S ORATORIOS

After Handel's Italianate operas grew out of favor with the public, he turned to writing oratorios. An oratorio is musically similar to an opera and employs the same trained singers as an opera, but an oratorio is non-staged, based on a religious theme. Oratorio places a greater emphasis on the chorus than opera. Hymn publishers found that oratorios were a more promising source of hymn tunes than operas.[51] The religious themes of oratorios also dispelled the criticism of borrowing hymn tunes from secular sources, including operas.

JUDAS MACCABEUS (or just MACCABEUS) was taken from the chorus "See, the conquering hero comes" in Handel's oratorio *Judas Maccabeus* (1747). Handel also used the tune in his oratorio *Joshua* (1747). When it was first conscripted as a hymn tune in *Harmonia Sacra* (1754), it was renamed ABINGTON.[52] The Wesleys used it in *Sacred Harmony* (1780) and called it MACCABEES, set to "Christ the Lord is ris'n today."

In Handel's oratorio *Theodora* (1755), a Christian girl refuses to sacrifice to Jove. The hymn tune THEODORA is from the song "Blessed be the pow'r who gave us." In the British Methodist *Hymns and Psalms* (1983), no. 759, this serves as the setting for Charles Wesley's "Jesus, Lord, we look to thee."

The hymn tune HALIFAX is derived from Handel's oratorio *Susanna* (1749), from the air "Ask if yon damask rose be sweet." It was given hymn tune status in the 1767 edition of Butts's *Harmonia Sacra*. In recent collections, it can be found in the Episcopal *Hymnal 1982*, nos. 459 & 629, the *Presbyterian Hymnal* (1990), nos. 167 & 556, and the *Trinity Psalter Hymnal* (2018), nos. 9A & 10. The tune itself is in doubled common meter (8.6.8.6.D). Its texture is folksong-like and is similar to a *bourée*. The bass of the light accompaniment is sometimes filled out or lowered an octave.

Other examples of hymn tunes drawn from oratorios are SOLOMON, SAMSON, DAVID, and THATCHER. SOLOMON is a hymn tune based on the aria "What tho' I trace," from Handel's oratorio *Solomon*. In the 1933 *Methodist Hymn-Book*, it was sung with Charles Wesley's "Father of Jesus Christ, my Lord." SAMSON is often set to either Isaac Watts' "Awake, our souls; away, our fears," or James Montgomery's "Come let us sing the song of songs." DAVID, from the oratorio *Sosarme*, was set to Charles Wesley's "Rejoice for a brother deceased" in the 1933 *Methodist Hymn-Book*.

---

51. Wilson, "Handel and the Hymn Tune: II," 26.
52. Wilson, "Handel and the Hymn Tune: II," 25.

THATCHER (1732) is very similar to DAVID; it has been paired with several different texts, including Charles Wesley's "Soldiers of Christ, arise," in the *African Methodist Episcopal Hymn and Tune Book* (1898).

MESSIAH

There are several hymn tunes based on Handel's ever-popular oratorio, *Messiah*. Although Handel's *Messiah* was enthusiastically received in its own day, hymn tunes derived from the work were "seldom successful because Messiah texts weren't metrical but were prose from the Bible and the melodies have the freedom associated with prose."[53] A few of the most successful adaptations are worth mentioning here.

The tune of the soprano aria "He shall feed his flock," usually called MANNING, appeared in John Rippon's *A Selection of Psalm and Hymn Tunes* (1792) with Isaac Watts' text, "When I survey the wondrous cross." The soprano aria "I know that my Redeemer liveth" has been adapted as the tune BRADFORD (or MESSIAH). It is sometimes set to Charles Wesley's "I know that my Redeemer lives," a pairing made as early as ca. 1785 in Aaron Williams' *British Psalmody*.[54]

The hymn tune ANTIOCH, often erroneously attributed to Handel or Lowell Mason, has melodic features resembling the opening instrumental strains of "Comfort ye" and the descending choral lines of "Glory to God" and/or "Lift up your heads," especially in the earliest printings of the tune. The tune was first published in Charles Rider's *Psalmodia Britannica*, vol. 4 (ca. 1831), said to be "Partly from J. Leach" and called COMFORT. It was first attributed to Handel in William Holford's *Voce di Melodia* (ca. 1833–1834). Lowell Mason introduced it to American audiences in *Occasional Psalm and Hymn Tunes* (1836), where it was called ANTIOCH, "Arranged from Handel," and set to Isaac Watts' "Joy to the world."[55] Although the tune echoes melodic turns from *Messiah*, it uses only brief segments and is not a proper parody or *contrafactum*.

---

53. Wilson, "Handel and the Hymn Tune: II," 26.

54. While it might be tempting to consider Wesley's hymn to be an adaptation of the aria from *Messiah*, Wesley's text was first published in *Hymns and Sacred Poems* (1742), released in late December 1741, whereas *Messiah* premiered 13 April 1742. The connection between text and tune was not made until 40 years later. In the 1780 *Collection*, this text was assigned to the tune LIVERPOOL.

55. For a more detailed history of the earliest printings of ANTIOCH/COMFORT, see Fenner, "Joy to the world," in *Hymnology Archive*.

CONCLUSION

Handel and many other composers, such as Purcell, Arne, Battishill, and Carey, exerted a clear operatic influence over the hymn tunes used by the Wesleys. This use of the operatic idiom popular at the time of the Wesleys was passed down to the modern church in less ornamented arrangements with written-out bass parts and fuller harmonizations. The largest contribution to operatic influences in Wesleyan hymnody was the twenty-four tunes in *Hymns on the Great Festivals* (1746) by composer and Methodist convert John Frederick Lampe, although only two of his hymn tunes remain in common use today.

Perhaps the largest contributor of operatic influence on the hymn tunes used by the Wesleys was Mrs. Rich. If she had not introduced London's prominent composers to the Wesleys, they might not have written such artistic melodies suitable for Charles's descriptive and varied texts, and the brothers might not have been as inclined to borrow other tunes for their tunebooks. It was a beautiful meeting, surely orchestrated by the Holy Spirit.

14

A Baptist preacher and a Methodist hymnal

Jim Scott Orrick

Sometime in the early 1980s, I was exploring the countryside not far from Richmond, Kentucky, when I came across an old abandoned Methodist church building. What had once been the yard around the building was grown up with brush and with trees large enough to indicate no one had used the building for a very long time. The structure was in severe disrepair. I made my way through the undergrowth and went in. Broken glass littered the floor, and the boards on the floor were curling up from exposure to the elements.

In a corner of the building still under roof, I found what had been a stack of hymnals. Bound in faded blue cloth, the covers bore the title *The Methodist Hymnal*.[1] Rats and mice had eaten most of them, but there was one the rodents had left alone. It was worn around the edges, and it had clearly been thoroughly used, but it was still in fair condition. I surmised that since the Methodists had not kept the mice from eating the other hymnals, perhaps they would not mind if a young Baptist preacher took the last one to use in his private devotions. I left a note with my contact information saying I had taken the hymnal, just in case anyone ever came looking for it. I have it on the desk in front of me as I type these words.

---

1. *The Methodist Hymnal* (Cincinnati: Methodist Publishing House, 1932).

That hymnal was a gold mine to me. I spent many hours reading the texts, singing the hymns I knew, and trying to figure out the tunes to the ones I did not know. In that hymnal I discovered Thomas Tiplady's hymn "Above the hills of time." It was set to the tune of Londonderry Aire, and it is a text worthy of that haunting, wistful melody. It remains one of my favorite hymns, and I would not mind if someone sang it to me when I am lying on my deathbed.

When I found the hymnal, it was my custom to sing a hymn when I awoke in the morning before I got out of bed, and I would sing another just before I went to sleep at night. Like many other older hymnals, my Methodist hymnal has sections devoted to morning hymns and evening hymns. I do not know how many mornings I have sung "When morning gilds the skies." Many nights, just before closing my eyes, I have sung "Savior, breathe an evening blessing" or "All praise to Thee my God this night." I learned them from the Methodist hymnal.

About that same time, I was listening to some old crackly recordings of George W. Truett, the most famous Southern Baptist preacher of the first half of the twentieth century. Besides being a powerful preacher, Truett was a lover of good literature, and he would sometimes very effectively quote poetry in his sermons. One such poem was Norman Macleod's "Courage brother! Do not stumble." I memorized the poem, and I have tried to make the refrain of that poem the guide for my life and ministry: "Trust in God, and do the right!" That poem is a hymn in the Methodist hymnal, number 298. Just as powerful, on the next page is Charles Wesley's "I want a principle within." As I recall, I resolved to commit that text to memory the very first time I saw it. I did so, and I have sung it over and over through the years, although I have never had the joy of singing it with others. The very next hymn, number 300, is Maltbie D. Babcock's "Be strong, we are not here to play, to dream, to drift." Three hymns in a row with the potential to inspire courage, fortitude, and integrity. What it would do to have these hymns ringing in a young man's ears and in his heart as he faces temptation and as he marches to battle beneath the banner of the cross! These hymns, and many like them, have colored my soul. I read these hymns today, remembering what they have meant to me, and I feel afresh the anguish of knowing how we have traded vast islands of riches for a pocket full of glass beads—mindless, powerless ditties, which will be swapped out next year for something just as ephemeral and just as superficial.

I must confess that not all the swapping has been for glass beads and mindless ditties. There have been many worthy, substantial songs composed for the church in recent years. What we seem to have done, however, is to trade a big treasure chest full of rubies, emeralds, sapphires, opals, and diamonds (to mention no more) for a much smaller treasure chest, having fewer varieties of precious jewels. Older hymnbooks, with their broad scope of hymns, offered the opportunity to sing about many aspects of the Christian faith and various Christian experiences. Without the guidance and suggestions offered by hymnbooks, we face the danger that as we teach and admonish one another in our singing, we will not explore the rich variety of Christian doctrine or the varied experiences of the Christian life.

Let me illustrate. In my *Methodist Hymnal*, out of 650 hymns, there are forty-five texts written by Charles Wesley. That is nearly three times as many texts as taken from Isaac Watts, who holds second place in the *Methodist Hymnal*. I stand in awe of Wesley's prolific output of hymns, and the way many of those hymns have lasted. Wesley died in 1788; this *Methodist Hymnal* was copyrighted in 1932. Nearly 150 years after his death, his hymns constituted around seven percent of a denominational hymnal. During his lifetime (1707–1788) he produced over fifty volumes of hymns in fifty-three years. He wrote over 6,000 hymns.[2]

During the eighteenth century revival, Charles's older brother John was often considered the most popular and influential of the two. But let me ask you, reader, have you ever read one of John Wesley's books? He produced a jaw-dropping amount of literature on an astounding array of topics. Can you name even one? Have you ever read even one of his sermons? On the other hand, more than 200 years after Charles died, we still sing several of his hymns, and they are among the best-loved hymns in Christianity. I have read all forty-five of Charles Wesley's hymn texts in my *Methodist Hymnal*. I have never heard most of them sung, but at least seven of them are among the most well-known hymns in Christendom, including "Hark! the herald angels sing," "Christ the Lord is ris'n today," and "Jesu, lover of my soul."

I am particularly impressed with two features of Wesley's hymns. First, he wrote on an amazing variety of topics.[3] In my *Methodist Hymnal* there are Wesley hymns to be used for specific times and occasions: beginning public worship, for meeting at church and for parting from church, for singing in the morning, for singing at Christmas, the New Year, and at Easter. There are hymns addressing specific theological issues: conversion,

---

2. The index of first lines compiled by Randy L. Maddox for the "Research Resources" page of his online edition lists 4,601 hymns by Charles, but some are listed twice ("Glory to God and praise and love" and "O for a thousand tongues to sing" are both given an entry, for example); Kimbrough and Beckerlegge compiled an additional 1,475 unpublished texts in three volumes of *The Unpublished Poetry of Charles Wesley*, not all of which are hymns. See the prefaces to those volumes for more explanation of what had already been published.

3. I refer to a number of hymns in what follows. I identify all of them in a list at the end.

sanctification, regeneration, and evangelism. There are hymns reflecting Wesleyan theological perspectives on Christian perfectionism and one on the despair felt by someone who has fallen from grace. There are a variety of hymns on Christian duty: not only the duties of prayer and fellowship, but there is a hymn to be sung before going to work in the morning ("Forth in Thy name, O Lord, I go"). It is this variety of topics I had in mind when I wrote above how we have traded a treasure chest full of differing jewels for a much smaller chest filled with fewer kinds of jewels. I hesitate to mention the very limited subject matter of the church songs I hear today, for the case can often be made that what we are singing about is important, and maybe it is even most important. But the city of God has more than one skyscraper. The garden of God has more than one flower. Or think of it this way: the vast soaring tower of the gospel is buttressed by a delightful array of supporting doctrines. I fear we have tried to strip the gospel down to its bare essentials, and then we sing about only those essentials. Can you get to heaven without singing a song dedicating your workday to God? Of course you can, but how much richer life is when you dedicate yourself to work like a Christian every day. Consider the stunning array of topics addressed in the Psalms, all of which were written by men living under the Old Covenant. Perhaps the outstanding feature of the Old Covenant was God's deliverance of Israel from Egyptian bondage, and taking them to be his own people, he now dwelt among them. Maybe you think the outstanding feature of the Old Covenant was something else. But whatever you identify as the outstanding feature, many of the Psalms are not directly about that outstanding feature. Rather, they are reflections and prescriptions and observations about the way things were or the way things ought to be, or how God's people ought to live in light of that outstanding feature. I am making a similar argument for variety in Christian hymnody.

There is no question about how the primary feature of the New Covenant is the work of Jesus—God's Son and God's appointed Savior—who has done everything necessary to reconcile sinners to God. The resurrected Christ is now reigning and subduing everything to himself. All those who repent of sin and receive Christ will be saved from sin and reign with Christ forever. If we can sing only one song, let it be this song. But we are not limited to one song. If you have a one-string banjo, let it be this string. But when possible, put a whole set of strings on your banjo. Following the example of the Psalms, Christian hymnody ought to reflect and prescribe and observe the way things are, or the way things ought to be, or how God's people ought to live in light of the gospel. With good intention, someone might ask, "How is a song about going to work about the Gospel?" Answer: It is about how Christian people live under the reign of Christ. "How is a song about bravery or courage about Christ?" Answer: It is a description of how Christ affects the character of his people and how we ought to live under his reign. We are to teach and admonish one another in our singing. What if all the teaching we ever received was through the songs we sang in public worship? I strongly suspect, in fact, the average church member learns most of his or her theology from the songs we sing in public worship.

I grew up in a church that met three times a week. At each of those services, we began with half an hour of singing from the hymnal. That is an hour and a half of hymn-singing every week. As a result, I had committed hundreds of hymns to memory without even trying! Church was not the only place I sang hymns. We sang hymns at home. My father and I would often sing hymns together by the hour while we were travelling. Hymns were part of my private devotions, and when I became a husband and father, hymns were part of our family devotions. The Psalms and Wesley's hymns reflect a time when people sang much more often than we do today. During the middle ages, French secular songs were about three main topics: love, the Crusades, and spinning. Spinning! That is, turning wool or flax into useable thread or yarn. Why spinning? Roughly half the population was spending a big part of their lives spinning. They were not listening to the radio when they were doing it. They were singing songs about spinning. I have no doubt blacksmiths had songs about smithing. Sailors had songs about sailing. Cobblers had songs about making shoes. They wanted to seek God's blessing on a great variety of activities. They wanted to praise God for a great variety of blessings and doctrines. Have you ever felt like you needed a good song to sing before going to bed? How about before setting out on your commute into work, or arriving home safely from your commute? If not, why not? Clearly, Charles Wesley believed the Christian life called for a wide variety of hymns to help us live all aspects of our lives under God's loving, watchful eye, in a conscious manner.

A second impressive feature of Wesley's hymns is the unity of the various texts. A song about conversion is about conversion from beginning to end. A song about the Holy Spirit is about the Holy Spirit from beginning to end. There are no sudden, puzzling references to the resurrection. There are no interpolations of impressive-sounding (but irrelevant) religious jargon. You could diagram all his sentences if you were so inclined. You can even identify sentences! I am tempted to say *most*, but I'll just say *many* of today's church songs have sections that are not cohesive with the rest of the song, where the song writers have inserted religious words and incoherent phrases. I love to sing, and I try to enter into the attitude suggested by the song we are singing, but I often find myself asking, "What does that phrase mean?" or "Why is that word there?" You may be sure there is no artificial food coloring in Wesley's hymns. Every phrase—every word—was skillfully chosen and it is saturated with meaning.

Some of Wesley's hymns have suffered at the hands of editorial hacks, and some have suffered just because congregations today do not want to sing all the stanzas of a hymn. I mentioned how one of the hymns in my *Methodist Hymnal* is about the misery of falling from grace: "O how happy are they who the Savior obey." Some well-meaning editor rightfully surmised that no one wants to sing about falling from grace, so he included only the first five stanzas, which describe the apostate's bliss before he apostatized. The problem is, the first five stanzas are phrased so as to make it plain that the bliss of which the poet speaks is a bliss entirely in the past. The thoughtful reader is left asking, "So what happened?" The doleful answer is given in the succeeding eleven stanzas, which are not published. Nonetheless, even for patient, persevering congregations, some of Wesley's compositions are too long to be sung in public. Almost as soon as the hymns were published, editors sometimes adopted some means of designating which stanzas might be omitted without damaging the meaning of the text. (It was not leaving out the third stanza.) "O for a thousand tongues to sing" has eighteen stanzas, and the stanzas we sing are enriched and informed by the ones we have never sung. I wonder if any congregation has ever sung all eighteen stanzas and enjoyed doing it. By the way, "O for a thousand tongues" is a hymn composed to be sung on the anniversary of one's conversion. What a great idea!

While Wesley wrote some hymns he probably knew were too long to sing in church, it is apparent he was usually writing hymns intended to be sung, not poems meant to be read. I think he is probably the most skilled poet of the great hymn writers, but while some sections of his hymns are great poetry, few of his entire hymns deserve to be regarded as great poetry. I am confident he was not trying to write great poetry. I love George Herbert's poetry, but from all of his sacred poems, not one has been transferred into a hymn which comes close to the popularity of Wesley's hymns. Really great poetry has an innate music, but really great poetry almost never sings well. Sometimes it can be crammed into church clothes, but they rarely look natural. I have read how the extremely learned John Owen once said he would gladly trade all his learning if he could preach like John Bunyan, the tinker. John Wesley gets attention, but Charles Wesley gets sung. It is no wonder. His hymns are useful for a variety of situations and seasons, they are solid, cohesive statements of truth and aspiration, and they have now acquired the charm of age.

I do not know anything about the people who once worshiped in the old dilapidated building that yielded up my *Methodist Hymnal*. I wonder if any of them are alive. But as they served the Lord Christ, their work was not in vain. I know their investment in hymnals continues to produce fruit in my life. I recently revived the practice of singing hymns in the morning and in the evening in my private devotions. Some of the hymns I sing are from the *Methodist Hymnal*. Someone once gave me a handmade hunting knife, which is valued at hundreds of dollars. It is a beautiful thing, but I do not carry it into the woods. I leave it at home in the safe. I would feel horrible if I lost a five-hundred-dollar knife! Instead, I usually use a knife I picked up at a yard sale for two dollars. It is a good knife, it does a variety of jobs, and I have been using it for nearly forty years! The hymns of Charles Wesley are much like that two-dollar knife. No doubt Charles will always be known as John Wesley's brother, but while John's sermons and books are carefully preserved in libraries and book shelves, Charles's hymns are sung every day by untold numbers of Christians.

Hymns by Charles Wesley described in this essay, implicitly and explicitly:

1. Beginning worship: "Jesus, we look to thee."
2. Meeting at church: "And are we yet alive?"
3. Parting from one another: "And let our bodies part."
4. Singing in the morning: "Christ, whose glory fills the skies."
5. Christmas: "Come, thou long expected Jesus," and "Hark, the herald angels sing."
6. New Year: "Come, let us anew our journey pursue," and "Sing to the great Jehovah's praise."
7. Resurrection: "Christ the Lord is ris'n today."
8. Conversion: "O for a thousand tongues to sing."
9. Sanctification: "Jesus, my strength, my hope," and "I want a principle within."
10. Regeneration: "O for a heart to praise my God," and "Jesus, thine all victorious love."
11. Evangelism: "Come, sinners to the gospel feast," and "Sinners, turn, why will ye die?"
12. Christian perfection: "Jesus, thine all victorious love," and "Love divine, all loves excelling."
13. Falling from grace: "O how happy are they who the Savior obey."
14. Prayer: "Come, O thou traveller unknown."

15. Fellowship: "Blest be the dear uniting love."
16. Holy Spirit: "Come Holy Ghost, our hearts inspire," and "Spirit of Faith, come down."
17. Spiritual distress: "Jesu, lover of my soul."
18. Christian life and work: "Forth in Thy name, O Lord, I go."

Appendix

A Collection of Tunes as They Were Used by the Wesleys

EDITED WITH COMMENTARY BY CHRIS FENNER

In their lifetimes, the Wesleys published four collections of hymn tunes. The first was *A Collection of Tunes, Set to Music, As They Are Commonly Sung at the Foundery* (1742), a set of forty-three tunes, melody only. *Hymns on the Great Festivals* (1746) contained a set of twenty-four tunes, all composed by John Frederick Lampe (1703–1751) for texts by Charles. Lampe's settings were for melody and figured bass. This collection was reprinted in 1753.

The next tune book compilation was appended to *Select Hymns with Tunes Annext* (1761), including 102 tunes, melody only. In the preface, John Wesley expressed his biggest concern in producing the volume:

> I have been endeavouring for more than twenty years to procure such a book as this. But in vain: masters of music were above following any direction but their own. And I was determined, whoever compiled this, should follow my direction: not mending our tunes, but setting them down, neither better nor worse than they were. At length I have prevailed. The following collection contains all the tunes which are in common use among us.

They are pricked true, exactly as I desire all our congregations may sing them.

This volume, then, is an accurate representation of what the Wesleys were singing. John also included his famous directions on how to sing congregationally, plus a rudimentary introduction to music reading. This collection was revised and expanded in 1765, containing 112 tunes, with an intermediate title page, *Sacred Melody*; this version was reprinted in 1770 (3rd ed.) and 1773 (4th ed.).

The Wesleys produced their last major tune book in 1780, *Sacred Harmony*. This collection contained 119 tunes, mostly melody and bass, with an occasional third harmony voice. This was printed again circa 1790, minus one tune.

One other volume contained music, *A Collection of Hymns and Sacred Poems* (1749), with 22 tunes, melody and bass. This collection was printed in Dublin, possibly edited by Lampe, not by the Wesleys.

Some of the Wesleys' textual collections included tune recommendations. *Graces Before and After Meat* (1746) suggested tunes for most of the texts, as did *Hymns for Those that Seek* (1747). *A Collection of Hymns for the Use of the People Called Methodists* contained tune recommendations, starting with the 5th ed. (1786), as did *A Pocket Hymn Book* (1785, rev. 1787).

Many of these tunes use grace notes. In the 18th century, a grace note displaced the following note, on the beat, rather than acting as a pickup note before the beat. For example, the first line of HOTHAM (no. 4), was printed like this:

In the Wesleys' time, the music would be sung like this:

1. Where shall my wond'ring soul begin? : In the 1780 *Collection* (eds. 5–7), the Wesleys recommended the tune FRANKFORT. The Wesleys used this tune in their *Foundery* collection (1742), where it was called SWIFT GERMAN TUNE and set to "Father of light, from whom proceeds," by Charles, from *Hymns and Sacred Poems* (1739). The tune was repeated in *Select Hymns* (1761) and *Sacred Harmony* (1780), renamed FRANKFORT, set to

"Father of light." This melody is from *Musicalisch Hand-Buch der Geistlichen Melodien à Cant. et Bass* (Hamburg, 1690; see Zahn 2781). The Wesleys were responsible for introducing this tune to English worshipers; they adapted it to fit the meter of this text.

2. And can it be that I should gain : This text appeared in the *Foundery* collection (1742) with CRUCIFIXION TUNE, by Samuel Akeroyde (fl.1684–1706). The Wesleys did not use this tune in subsequent tunebooks. In the 1780 *Collection* (eds. 5–7), the recommended tune was BIRMINGHAM, which appeared in *Select Hymns* (1761) and *Sacred Harmony* (1780) with "Thou hidden source of calm repose," by Charles, from *Hymns and Sacred Poems*, vol. 1 (1749). The author of the tune is unknown. In 1754, it had been printed in *Divine Musical Miscellany* (a tunebook for George Whitefield's congregation), and in Thomas Butts' *Harmonia-Sacra*.

3. O for a thousand tongues to sing : In the 1780 *Collection* (eds. 5–7), the recommended tune was BIRSTAL. The Wesleys had used this tune in *Select Hymns* (1761) and *Sacred Harmony* (1780) with "Thee we adore, eternal name" by Isaac Watts, from his *Hymns and Spiritual Songs* (1707). The Wesleys were the first to print this tune in 1761. The author is unknown.

4. Jesu, lover of my soul : In the revised edition of *Select Hymns* (1765) and in *Sacred Harmony* (1780), this text was set to HOTHAM, a tune by Martin Madan, from *A Collection of Psalm and Hymn Tunes* (ca. 1760–1763); Madan had also set it to this text.

5. Come, O thou traveller unknown : In the *Foundery* collection (1742), this text was set to CARDIFF. The tune is of unknown origin and was first published in this collection. The Wesleys used this tune in *Select Hymns* (1761) and *Sacred Harmony* (1780), except they changed the name to WELCH and reassigned the text to "O love divine, what hast thou done?" by Charles, from *Hymns and Sacred Poems* (1742). In the 1780 *Collection* (eds. 5–7), the recommended tune for "Come, O thou traveller unknown" was TRAVELLER. Curiously, in spite of the obvious name connection, this tune had been set to "Come on, my partners in distress" in both *Select Hymns*, rev. ed. (1765) and *Sacred Harmony* (1780). In these tune books, the melody was designed to fit texts of 8.8.6.8.8.6, but it can be made to fit the longer 8.8.8.8.8.8 of "Come, O thou traveller unknown." TRAVELLER is based on Henry Holcombe's song "A Thought in a Grotto," which had been published in *The Musical Medley* (1755).

6. Come, thou long-expected Jesus : Among the numerous Wesleyan collections, this text was only printed in *Nativity Hymns*, not repeated in any of their larger compilations. *Nativity Hymns* did not include tune data. In John

Rippon's influential *Selection of Psalm and Hymn Tunes* (1792), this hymn was set to WELSH, a tune of unknown origins. This tune was known to the Wesleys, included in the revised edition of *Select Hymns* (1765), where it was called ST. PETER'S and set to "Jesu, help thy fallen creature," a text by Charles from *Hymns and Sacred Poems*, vol. 2 (1749). ST. PETER'S was not included in *Sacred Harmony* (1780); the only tune in that collection suitable for 8.7.8.7.D trochaic was WESTMINSTER (see No. 11, "Love divine, all loves excelling").

7. Hark! the herald angels sing : In the revised edition of *A Pocket Hymn Book* (1787), the Wesleys recommended the tune SALISBURY for this hymn. In Wesleyan collections, the tune was modified from the way it had originally appeared in *Lyra Davidica* (1708). The Wesleys started using this tune in the *Foundery* collection (1742) with "Christ the Lord is risen today" (see no. 8). In the 1749 Dublin *Collection*, this tune was simply labeled Hymn 54 and was paired with "Hark, how all the welkin rings." In *Select Hymns* (1761) and *Sacred Harmony* (1780), this tune was paired with "Glory be to God on high," a text by Charles from *Hymns and Sacred Poems* (1739).

8. Christ the Lord is ris'n today : This text was first published with music in the *Foundery* collection (1742), with the tune SALISBURY, adapted from *Lyra Davidica* (1708). In *Select Hymns* (1761) and *Sacred Harmony* (1780), this tune was paired with "Glory be to God on high," a text by Charles from *Hymns and Sacred Poems* (1739). In *Sacred Harmony* (1780), "Christ the Lord is ris'n today" was set to MACCABEES, a tune taken from the chorus "See, the conquering hero comes" in Handel's oratorio *Judas Maccabeus* (1747). This was first adapted as a hymn tune in Thomas Butts' *Harmonia Sacra* (1754), where it was named ABINGTON and set to "Christ the Lord is ris'n today."

9. The Means of Grace : In the 1780 *Collection* (eds. 5–7), the recommended tune for this hymn was FETTER LANE, by Adam Krieger (1634–1666), from the German hymn "Nun sich der Tag geendet hat." The Wesleys had used this tune in the *Foundery* collection (1742), but called it MARIENBORN and set it to "Enslav'd to sense, to pleasure prone," a text by Charles from *Hymns and Sacred Poems* (1739). In *Select Hymns* (1761), the Wesleys changed the name of MARIENBORN to FETTER LANE and set it to "How sad our state by nature is!" That combination was repeated in *Sacred Harmony* (1780). A different, unrelated tune called FETTER LANE in the 1742 collection is of unknown origins, dating as early as 1717 in English collections.

10. O the depth of love divine : This hymn was only published in *Hymns on the Lord's Supper* (1745), without tune information. Given the unique meter of 7.6.7.6.7.7.7.6, very few tunes would be suitable, but the Wesleys had one such tune in their repertoire: AMSTERDAM. They were the first to print this tune in English, in the *Foundery* collection (1742), where it was set to "I will hearken what my Lord," a text by Charles from *Hymns and Sacred Poems* (1742). The tune is adapted from Johann Georg Hille (d. 1744), originally associated with the German text "Sei willkommen, sei willkommen, Jesulein, mein Freund." In Wesleyan collections, this tune was repeated in *Select Hymns* (1761) and *Sacred Harmony* (1780), set to "God of unexampled grace," another text by Charles from *Hymns on the Lord's Supper* (1745).

11. Love divine, all loves excelling : This hymn was a Christianized parody of a song from the opera *King Arthur*, Act II, Scene 5, "Fairest Isle, all isles excelling," words by John Dryden (1631–1700), with music by Henry Purcell (1659–1695). The Wesleys adapted this tune for *Select Hymns* (1761) and *Sacred Harmony* (1780), and called it WESTMINSTER. In spite of the clear connection to Dryden and Purcell, the first printing of "Love divine" in 1747 was paired with a tune by John Frederick Lampe, written for *Hymns on the Great Festivals* (1746). Lampe's tune was intended for "Jesu, show us thy salvation," by Charles, from *Hymns for Our Lord's Resurrection* (1746).

12. Sun of Unclouded Righteousness : In the 1780 *Collection* (eds. 5–7), this text was paired with MARIENBOURN, which is an adaptation of the tune BREMEN by Georg Christian Neumark (1621–1681), from the German hymn "Wer nur den lieben Gott lässt walten." The tune appeared in the *Foundery* collection (1742), named SLOW GERMAN, and set to "My Father, O my Father, hear," a text by Charles from *Hymns and Sacred Poems* (1742). In *Select Hymns* (1761) and *Sacred Harmony* (1780), it was renamed MARIENBOURN and set to "Lo, God is here; let us adore," a translation by John from "Gott is gegenwärtig," by Gerhardt Tersteegen (1697–1769); the translation first appeared in *Hymns and Sacred Poems* (1739). See the confusion of tune names between this and FETTER LANE, no. 9 above.

13a. Thou Shepherd of Israel, and mine : This tune is by Thomas Arne (1710–1778), adapted from the aria "Waters parted from the sea" in his opera *Artaxerxes* (1762). This was first printed as a hymn tune in Thomas Knibb, *The Psalm Singers Help* (n.d.) and called MITCHAM. The Wesleys incorporated it into the revised edition of *Select Hymns* (1765) and called it THE SHEPHERD OF ISRAEL, set to Charles's text, "Thou shepherd of Israel, and mine." In *Sacred Harmony* (1780), the name was changed to SALTERS for unknown reasons. This text first appeared in *Short Hymns on Select*

Passages of the Holy Scriptures, vol. 1 (1762), based on Song of Solomon 1:7 ("Tell me, O thou whom my soul loveth, where thou feedest, where thou makest thy flock to rest at noon," KJV).

13b. He comes! he comes! the judge severe : This tune is by Henry Carey (ca. 1692–1743), adapted from the song "He comes! he comes! the hero comes!" written to commemorate the capture of Portobello, Panama, in 1739, by Admiral Edward Vernon. Similar to "Love divine, all loves excelling" (see no. 11), Charles wrote this parody for Christian purposes, first publishing his text in *Hymns of Intercession* (1758). John published this text and tune in *Select Hymns* (1761) and *Sacred Harmony* (1780), calling the tune JUDGMENT.

13c. Sinners, obey the gospel word : This text by Charles Wesley and this tune by John Frederick Lampe both appeared for the first time in *Hymns on the Great Festivals* (1746). This pairing was repeated in *A Collection of Hymns and Sacred Poems* (1749), *Select Hymns* (1761), and *Sacred Harmony* (1780).

13d. Soldiers of Christ, arise : This tune is adapted from a march in Act III of *Riccardo Primo* (1727) by George Frideric Handel (1685–1759). It was used by the Wesleys in the *Foundery* collection (1742), called JERICHO and set to John's "Commit thou all thy griefs," a translation of the German hymn "Befiehl du deine Wege" by Paul Gerhardt (1607–1676). In *Select Hymns* (1761) and *Sacred Harmony* (1780), it was called HANDEL'S MARCH and set to Charles's text "Soldiers of Christ, arise," from a broadsheet of hymns titled *The Whole Armour of God* (1742).

14. I want a principle within : In the 1780 *Collection* (eds. 5–7), this text was paired with WENVO. The tune was introduced to English worshipers by the Wesleys in the *Foundery* collection (1742), where it was set to "Oh, that thou would'st the heavens rend, in majesty come down" a text by Charles from *Hymns and Sacred Poems* (1742). The tune might be Welsh, named after a village near Cardiff. In *Select Hymns* (1761) and *Sacred Harmony* (1780), this tune was set to "From whence these dire portents around," by Charles, from *Hymns Occasioned by the Earthquake*, Part 1 (1750).

A Collection of Tunes as They Were Sung by the Wesleys

1. Where shall my wond'ring soul begin?

FRANKFORT by Georg Neumark, as in *Sacred Harmony* (1780); text by C.W., as in *Collection*, 2nd ed. (1781).

4. No, tho' the ancient dragon rage,
　　And call forth all his host to war,
　Tho' earth's self-righteous sons engage,
　　Them and their god alike I dare;
　Jesus, the sinner's friend, proclaim;
　Jesus, to sinners still the same.

5. Outcasts of men, to you I call,
　　Harlots, and publicans, and theives!
　He spreads his arms t' embrace you all;
　　Sinners alone his grace receives.
　No need of him the righteous have;
　He came the lost to seek and save.

6. Come, O my guilty brethren, come,
　　Groaning beneath your load of sin!
　His bleeding heart shall make you room,
　　His open side shall take you in;
　He calls you now, invites you home—
　Come, O my guilty brethren, come!

7. For you the purple current flowed,
　　In pardons from his wounded side;
　Languished for you th' eternal God;
　　For you the Prince of Glory died;
　Believe, and all your sin's forgiv'n;
　Only believe, and yours is heav'n!

2a. And can it be that I should gain

CRUCIFIXION TUNE by Samuel Akeroyde (fl. 1684–1706), as in the *Foundery* collection (1742).

2b. And can it be that I should gain

1. And can it be that I should gain An in-t'rest in the Sav-ior's blood? Died he for me, who caused his pain! For me! who him to death pur-sued.
2. 'Tis mys-t'ry all: th'I-mor-tal dies! Who can ex-plore his strange de-sign? In vain the first-born ser-aph tries To sound the depths of love di-vine.

3. He left his Father's throne above,
   (So free, so infinite His grace!)
   Emptied himself of all but love,
   And bled for Adam's helpless race:
   'Tis mercy all, immense and free,
   For O my God, it found out me!
   For O, for O, etc.

4. Long my imprisoned spirit lay,
   Fast bound in sin and nature's night;
   Thine eye diffused a quick'ning ray;
   I woke; the dungeon flamed with light!
   My chains fell off, my heart was free,
   I rose, went forth, and followed Thee.
   I rose, I rose, etc.

BIRMINGHAM by unknown (ca. 1754), as in *Sacred Harmony* (1780); text by C.W., as in the *Collection* (1780).

[5. Still the small inward voice I hear
  That whispers all my sins forgiv'n;
 Still th' atoning blood is near,
  That quench'd the wrath of hostile Heav'n.
 I feel the life his wounds impart;
 I feel my Saviour in my heart.
 I feel, I feel, etc.]

6. No condemnation now I dread;
  Jesus, and all in him, is mine;
 Alive in him, my living Head,
  And clothed in righteousness divine,
 Bold I approach th' eternal throne,
 And claim the crown, thru Christ, my own.
 And claim, and claim, etc.

3. O for a thousand tongues to sing

1. O for a thousand tongues to sing My dear Redeemer's praise! The glories of my God and King, The triumphs of his grace!

2. My gracious Master, and my God, Assist me to proclaim, To spread thru all the earth abroad The honours of thy name.

3. Jesus, the name that charms our fears, That bids our sorrows cease; 'Tis music in the sinner's ears, 'Tis life, and health, and peace.

4. He breaks the power of cancell'd sin,
   He sets the pris'ner free;
   His blood can make the foulest clean,
   His blood availed for me.

5. Hear him, ye deaf; his praise, ye dumb,
   Your loosen'd tongues employ;
   Ye blind, behold your Saviour come,
   And leap, ye lame, for joy!

6. Look unto him, ye nations own
   Your God, ye fallen race;
   Look, and be saved thru faith alone,
   Be justified by grace.

7. See all your sins on Jesus laid:
   The Lamb of God was slain;
   His soul was once an offering made
   For every soul of man.

8. Awake from guilty nature's sleep,
   And Christ shall give you light;
   Cast all your sins into the deep,
   And wash the [darkness] white.

9. With me your chief ye then shall know,
   Shall feel your sins forgiv'n;
   Anticipate your heav'n below,
   And own that love is heav'n.

BIRSTAL by unknown (1761), as in *Sacred Harmony* (1780); text by C.W., as in the *Collection* (1780).

4. Jesu, lover of my soul

1. Je - su, lov - er of my soul, Let me to thy bo - som fly, While the near - er wa - ters roll, While the tem - pest still is high; Hide me, O — my Sav - ior, hide, Till — the storm of — life is past; Safe in - to the hav - en guide; O re - ceive, O — re - ceive, O — re - ceive my soul at last.

2. Oth - er re - fuge have I none; Hangs my help - less soul on thee; Leave, ah! leave me not a - lone. Still sup - port and com - fort me. All — my trust on thee is — stay'd; All — my help from thee I bring; Cov - er my de - fence - less head With the — sha - dow, With the sha - dow, with the sha - dow of thy wing.

3. Wilt thou not re - gard my call? Wilt thou not ac - cept my pray'r? Lo! I sink, I faint, I fall; Lo! on — thee I cast my care. Reach me out thy gra - cious hand! While I — of — thy strength re - ceive, Hop - ing a - gainst hope I — stand, Dy - ing and, — Dy - ing and, — Dy - ing, and be - hold I live!

HOTHAM by Martin Madan, as in *Sacred Harmony* (1780); text by C.W., as in *A Pocket Hymn Book* (1785).

4. Thou, O Christ, art all I want,
    More than all in thee I find;
    Raise the fallen, cheer the faint,
    Heal the sick, and lead the blind.
Just and holy is thy name;
    I am all unrighteousness;
False and full of sin I am;
    Thou art full of truth and grace.

5. Plenteous grace with thee is found,
    Grace to cover all my sin;
    Let the healing streams abound;
    Make and keep me pure within.
Thou of life the fountain art;
    Freely let me take of thee;
Spring thou up within my heart;
    Rise to all eternity!

5a. Come, O thou traveller unknown

WELCH, by unknown, as in *Sacred Harmony* (1780); text by C.W., as in the *Collection* (1780).

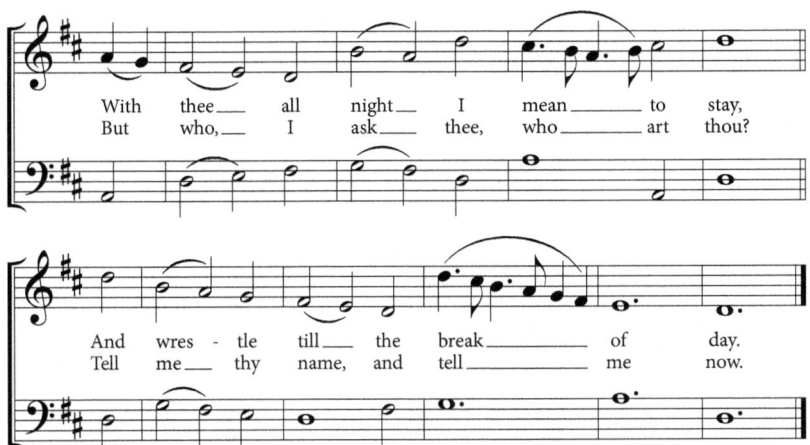

With thee all night I mean to stay,
And wres-tle till the break of day.

But who, I ask thee, who art thou?
Tell me thy name, and tell me now.

3. In vain thou strugglest to get free,
   I never will unloose my hold.
   Art thou the man that died for me?
   The secret of thy love unfold;
   Wrestling, I will not let thee go,
   Till I thy name, thy nature know.

4. Wilt thou not yet to me reveal
   Thy new, unutterable name?
   Tell me, I still beseech thee, tell,
   To know it now, resolv'd I am;
   Wrestling I will not let thee go,
   Till I thy name, thy nature know.

5. What though my shrinking flesh complain,
   And murmur to contend so long,
   I rise superior to my pain;
   When I am weak, then I am strong;
   And when my all of strength shall fail,
   I shall with the God-man prevail.

6. Yield to me now—for I am weak,
   But confident in self-despair!
   Speak to my heart, in blessings speak,
   Be conquer'd by my instant prayer;
   Speak, or thou never hence shalt move,
   And tell me, if thy name is love.

7. 'Tis love! 'tis love! thou diedst for me!
   I hear thy whisper in my heart.
   The morning breaks, the shadows flee:
   Pure UNIVERSAL LOVE thou art,
   To me, to all thy bowels move,
   Thy nature, and thy name is love.

8. My pray'r hath pow'r with God; the grace
   Unspeakable I now receive,
   Through faith I see thee face to face;
   I see thee face to face, and live!
   In vain I have not wept and strove;
   Thy nature, and thy name is love.

9. I know thee, Saviour, who thou art,
   Jesus, the feeble sinner's friend;
   Nor wilt thou with the night depart,
   But stay, and love me to the end;
   Thy mercies never shall remove,
   Thy nature, and thy name is love.

10. The Sun of Righteousness on me
    Hath rose, with healing in his wings;
    Wither'd my nature's strength; from thee
    My soul its life and succour brings;
    My help is all laid up above;
    Thy nature, and thy name is love.

11. Contented now, upon my thigh
    I halt, till life's short journey end;
    All helplesness, all weakness I,
    On thee alone for strength depend,
    Nor have I power from thee to move;
    Thy nature, and thy name is love.

12. Lame as I am, I take the prey,
    Hell, earth, and sin with ease o'ercome;
    I leap for joy, pursue my way,
    And as a bounding hart fly home,
    Through all eternity to prove
    Thy nature, and thy name is love.

5b. Come, O thou traveller unknown

1. Come, O thou traveller unknown, Whom still I hold, but cannot see! My company before is gone, And I am left alone with thee: With thee all night I mean to stay, and wrestle till the break of day.

2. I need not tell thee who I am, My misery or sin declare; Thyself hast call'd me by my name; Look on thy hands, and read it there! But who, I ask thee, who art thou? Tell me thy name, and tell me now.

TRAVELLER by Henry Holcombe, as in *Sacred Harmony* (1780); text by C.W., as in the *Collection* (1780).

3. In vain thou strugglest to get free,
    I never will unloose my hold.
Art thou the man that died for me?
    The secret of thy love unfold;
Wrestling, I will not let thee go,
Till I thy name, thy nature know.

4. Wilt thou not yet to me reveal
    Thy new, unutterable name?
Tell me, I still beseech thee, tell,
    To know it now, resolv'd I am;
Wrestling I will not let thee go,
Till I thy name, thy nature know.

5. What though my shrinking flesh complain,
    And murmur to contend so long,
I rise superior to my pain;
    When I am weak, then I am strong;
And when my all of strength shall fail,
I shall with the God-man prevail.

6. Yield to me now—for I am weak,
    But confident in self-despair!
Speak to my heart, in blessings speak,
    Be conquer'd by my instant prayer;
Speak, or thou never hence shalt move,
And tell me, if thy name is love.

7. 'Tis love! 'tis love! thou diedst for me!
    I hear thy whisper in my heart.
The morning breaks, the shadows flee:
    Pure UNIVERSAL LOVE thou art,
To me, to all thy bowels move,
Thy nature, and thy name is love.

8. My pray'r hath pow'r with God; the grace
    Unspeakable I now receive,
Through faith I see thee face to face;
    I see thee face to face, and live!
In vain I have not wept and strove;
Thy nature, and thy name is love.

9. I know thee, Saviour, who thou art,
    Jesus, the feeble sinner's friend;
Nor wilt thou with the night depart,
    But stay, and love me to the end;
Thy mercies never shall remove,
Thy nature, and thy name is love.

10. The Sun of Righteousness on me
    Hath rose, with healing in his wings;
Wither'd my nature's strength; from thee
    My soul its life and succour brings;
My help is all laid up above;
Thy nature, and thy name is love.

11. Contented now, upon my thigh
    I halt, till life's short journey end;
All helplesness, all weakness I,
    On thee alone for strength depend,
Nor have I power from thee to move;
Thy nature, and thy name is love.

12. Lame as I am, I take the prey,
    Hell, earth, and sin with ease o'ercome;
I leap for joy, pursue my way,
    And as a bounding hart fly home,
Through all eternity to prove
Thy nature, and thy name is love.

6. Come, thou long-expected Jesus

ST. PETER'S by unknown, as in *Select Hymns*, rev. (1765); text by C.W., as in *Nativity Hymns* (1777 ed.).
This text can also be sung to WESTMINSTER (see 11a).

7. Hark! the herald angels sing

SALISBURY from *Lyra Davidica* (1708), as in *Sacred Harmony* (1780);
text by C.W., as in *A Pocket Hymn Book*, rev. (1787).

"God and sin-ners re-con-ciled," hal - le-lu - jah!
"Christ is born in Beth-le-hem," hal - le-lu - jah!

2. Christ, by highest heav'n adored,
   Christ, the everlasting Lord;
   Late in time behold him come,
   Offspring of a virgin's womb;

   Veiled in flesh, the Godhead see;
   Hail th' incarnate Deity!
   Pleased as man with men t' appear,
   Jesus our Immanuel here.

3. Hail, the heav'n-born Prince of Peace,
   Hail, the Sun of Righteousness!
   Light and life to all he brings,
   Ris'n with healing in his wings;

   Mild he lays his glory by,
   Born that man no more may die,
   Born to raise the sons of earth,
   Born to give them second birth.

4. Come, desire of nations, come,
   Fix in us thy humble home;
   Rise, the woman's conq'ring seed;
   Bruise in us the serpent's head;

   Adam's likeness now efface;
   Stamp thine image in its place;
   Second Adam from above,
   Reinstate us in thy love.

8a. Christ the Lord is ris'n today

1. "Christ the Lord is ris'n to-day," hallelujah!
   Sons of men and angels say, hallelujah!
   Raise your joys and triumphs high, hallelujah!
   Sing ye heav'ns, and earth reply, hallelujah!

2. Love's redeeming work is done, hallelujah!
   Fought the fight, the battle won, hallelujah!
   Lo! our sun's eclipse is o'er, hallelujah!
   Lo! He sets in blood no more, hallelujah!

3. Vain the stone, the watch, the seal, hallelujah!
   Christ hath burst the gates of hell, hallelujah!
   Death in vain forbids his rise, hallelujah!
   Christ hath op'nd paradise, hallelujah!

4. Lives again our glorious King.
   Where, O death, is now thy sting?
   Once he died our souls to save.
   Where thy victory, O grave?

5. Soar we now, where Christ has led,
   Following our exalted Head;
   Made like him, like him we rise;
   Ours the cross, the grave, the skies.

6. What tho' once we perish'd all,
   Partners of our parent's fall,
   Second life we all receive,
   In our heav'nly Adam live.

7. Ris'n with him, we upward move;
   Still we seek the things above;
   Still pursue and kiss the Son,
   Seated on his Father's throne.

8. Scarce on earth a thought bestow,
   Dead to all we leave below;
   Heav'n our aim, and lov'd abode;
   Hid our life with Christ in God!

9. Hid, till Christ our life appear,
   Glorious in his members here;
   Join'd to him, we then shall shine,
   All immortal, all divine!

10. Hail the Lord of earth and heav'n!
    Praise to thee by both be giv'n;
    Thee we greet triumphant now;
    Hail the resurrection thou!

11. King of glory, soul of bliss,
    Everlasting life is this;
    Thee to know, thy pow'r to prove,
    Thus to sing, and thus to love!

SALISBURY from *Lyra Davidica* (1708), as in the *Foundery* collection (1742); text by C.W., as in *Hymns and Sacred Poems*, 4th ed. (1743).

MACCABEES by G.F. Handel, as in *Sacred Harmony* (1780);
text by C.W., as in *Hymns and Sacred Poems*, 4th ed. (1743).

2. Love's redeeming work is done;
   Fought the fight, the battle won;
   Lo! our sun's eclipse is o'er;
   Lo! He sets in blood no more.
   Lo! our sun's eclipse is o'er;
   Lo! He sets in blood no more.

3. Vain the stone, the watch, the seal;
   Christ hath burst the gates of hell!
   Death in vain forbids his rise;
   Christ hath open'd paradise!
   Death in vain forbids his rise;
   Christ hath open'd paradise!

4. Lives again our glorious King.
   Where, O death, is now thy sting?
   Once he died our souls to save.
   Where thy victory, O grave?
   Once he died our souls to save.
   Where thy victory, O grave?

5. Soar we now, where Christ has led,
   Following our exalted Head;
   Made like him, like him we rise;
   Ours the cross, the grave, the skies.
   Made like him, like him we rise;
   Ours the cross, the grave, the skies.

6. What tho' once we perish'd all,
   Partners of our parent's fall,
   Second life we all receive,
   In our heav'nly Adam live.
   Second life we all receive,
   In our heav'nly Adam live.

7. Ris'n with him, we upward move;
   Still we seek the things above;
   Still pursue and kiss the Son,
   Seated on his Father's throne.
   Still pursue and kiss the Son,
   Seated on his Father's throne.

8. Scarce on earth a thought bestow,
   Dead to all we leave below;
   Heav'n our aim, and lov'd abode;
   Hid our life with Christ in God!
   Heav'n our aim, and lov'd abode;
   Hid our life with Christ in God!

9. Hid, till Christ our life appear,
   Glorious in his members here;
   Join'd to him, we then shall shine,
   All immortal, all divine!
   Join'd to him, we then shall shine,
   All immortal, all divine!

10. Hail the Lord of earth and heav'n!
    Praise to thee by both be giv'n;
    Thee we greet triumphant now;
    Hail the resurrection thou!
    Thee we greet triumphant now;
    Hail the resurrection thou!

11. King of glory, soul of bliss,
    Everlasting life is this;
    Thee to know, thy pow'r to prove,
    Thus to sing, and thus to love!
    Thee to know, thy pow'r to prove,
    Thus to sing, and thus to love!

9. The Means of Grace

1. Long have I seem'd to serve thee, Lord, With unavailing pain; Fasted, and pray'd and read thy word, And heard it preach'd in vain.
2. Oft did I with th' assembly join, And near thy altar draw; A form of godliness was mine, The pow'r I never knew.
3. I rested in the outward law, Nor knew its deep design; The length and breadth I never saw, And height of love divine.

4. To please thee thus, at length I see,
   Vainly I hoped and strove;
   For what are outward things to thee,
   Unless they spring from love?

5. I see the perfect law requires
   Truth in the inward parts;
   Our full consent, our whole desires,
   Our undivided hearts.

6. But I of means have made my boast,
   Of means an idol made!
   The spirit in the letter lost,
   The substance in the shade!

7. Where am I now, or what my hope?
   What can my weakness do?
   Jesu, to thee my soul looks up;
   'Tis thou must make it new.

FETTER LANE by Adam Krieger, as in *Sacred Harmony* (1780); text by C.W., as in the *Collection*, 2nd ed. (1781).

10. O the depth of love divine

1. O the depth of love divine, Th' unfathomable grace re-
2. Let the wisest mortal show How we the
3. How can heav'nly spirits rise By earthly matter be un-
4. Sure and real is the grace, The manner

AMSTERDAM by Johann Georg Hille, as in *Sacred Harmony* (1780); text by C.W., as in *Hymns on the Lord's Supper* (1745).

11a. Love divine, all loves excelling

WESTMINSTER by Henry Purcell, as in *Sacred Harmony* (1780); text by C.W., as in the *Collection* (1780).

11b. Love divine, all loves excelling

HYMN IX by John Frederick Lampe, as in *Hymns on the Great Festivals* (1746); text by C.W., as in the *Collection* (1780).

12. Sun of unclouded righteousness

MARIENBOURN by Georg Neumark, as in *Sacred Harmony* (1780); text by C.W., as in the *Collection* (1780).

13a. Thou Shepherd of Israel and mine

SALTERS by Thomas Arne, as in *Sacred Harmony* (1780); text by C.W., as in *Short Hymns* (1762).

13b. He comes! he comes! the judge severe

1. He comes! he comes! the judge severe! The sev-enth trum-pet speaks him near; His light-nings flash, his tun-ders roll; How wel-come to the faith-ful soul. Wel-come, wel-come, wel-come, wel-come, wel-come to the faith-ful soul!
2. From heav'n an-gel-ic voic-es sound, See the al-might-y Je-sus crown'd! Girt with om-ni-po-tence and grace, And glo-ry decks the Sav-ior's face! Glo-ry, glo-ry, glo-ry, glo-ry, glo-ry decks the Sav-ior's face!
3. De-scend-ing on his a-zure throne, He claims the king-doms for his own; The king-doms all o-bey his word, And hail him their tri-um-phant Lord! Hail him, hail him, hail him, hail him, hail him their tri-um-phant Lord!
4. Shout all the peo-ple of the sky, And all the saints of the Most High; Our Lord, who now his right ob-tains, For ev-er and for ev-er reigns. Ev-er, ev-er, ev-er, ev-er, ev-er and for ev-er reigns!

JUDGMENT by Henry Carey, as in *Sacred Harmony* (1780); text by C.W., as in the *Collection* (1780).

13c. Sinners, obey the gospel word

1. Sinners, obey the gospel word!
Haste to the supper of my Lord;
Be wise to know your gracious day!
All things are ready; come away!

2. Ready the Father is to own,
And kiss his late returning son;
Ready your loving Savior stands,
And spreads for you his bleeding hands.

3. Ready the Spirit of his love,
Just now the stony to remove;
T' apply, and witness with the blood,
And wash, and seal the sons of God.

4. Ready for you the angels wait,
To triumph in your blest estate;
Tuning their harps, they long to praise
The wonders of redeeming grace.

5. The Father, Son, and Holy Ghost
Is ready with their shining host;
All heav'n is ready to resound,
"The dead's alive! The lost is found."

6. Come, then, ye sinners, to your Lord,
In Christ to paradise restored,
His proffer'd benefits embrace.
The plenitude of gospel-grace.

7. A pardon written with his blood,
The favour and the peace of God;
The seeing eye, the feeling sense,
The mystic joys of penitence:

8. The godly fear, the pleasing smart,
The meltings of a broken heart,
The tears that tell your sins forgiven,
The sighs that waft your souls to heav'n:

9. The guiltless shame, the sweet distress,
The unutterable tenderness,
The genuine, meek humility,
The wonder, "Why such love to me!"

10. The o'er whelming pow'r of saving grace,
The sight that veils the seraph's face
The speechless awe that dares not move,
And all the silent heav'n of love.

INVITATION by J.F. Lampe, as in *Sacred Harmony* (1780); text by C.W., as in the *Collection* (1780).

HANDEL'S MARCH by G.F. Handel, as in *Sacred Harmony* (1780); text by C.W., as in the *Collection* (1780).

14. I want a principle within

WENVO by unknown, as in *Sacred Harmony* (1780); text by C.W., as in the *Collection* (1780).

4. If to the right or left I stray,
    That moment, Lord, reprove;
  And let me weep my life away,
    For having grieved thy love,
    For having grieved,
    For having grieved thy love.

5. O may the least omission pain
    My well-instructed soul!
  And drive me to the blood again,
    Which makes the wounded whole.
    Which makes them whole,
    Which makes the wounded whole.

Bibliography

WESLEYAN HYMN COLLECTIONS (CHRONOLOGICAL)

A Collection of Psalms and Hymns. Charlestown: Lewis Timothy, 1737.
Hymns and Sacred Poems. London: William Strahan, 1739.
———. 2nd ed. London: William Strahan, 1739.
———. 4th ed. Bristol: Felix Farley, 1743.
Hymns and Sacred Poems. London: William Strahan, 1740.
Hymns and Sacred Poems. Bristol: Felix Farley, 1742.
A Collection of Hymns. London: William Strahan, 1742.
A Collection of Tunes, Set to Music, As They Are Commonly Sung at the Foundery. London: A. Pearson, 1742.
The Whole Armour of God. [Bristol: Felix Farley, 1742.]
Hymns for the Nativity of Our Lord. [London: William Strahan, 1745].
Hymns for the Lord's Supper. Bristol: Felix Farley, 1745.
Gloria Patri, etc. Or Hymns to the Trinity. London, 1746.
Hymns for Our Lord's Resurrection. London: William Strahan, 1746.
Hymns on the Great Festivals and Other Occasions. London: M. Cooper, 1746.
Graces Before and After Meat. Dublin: S. Powell, 1747.
Hymns and Sacred Poems. Dublin, 1747.
Hymns for Those that Seek and Those that Have Redemption in the Blood of Jesus Christ. Bristol: Felix Farley, 1747.
A Collection of Hymns and Sacred Poems. Dublin: S. Powell, 1749.
Hymns and Sacred Poems. 2 vols. Bristol: Felix Farley, 1749.
Hymns Occasioned by the Earthquake. Part 1. London, 1750.
Hymns and Spiritual Songs. London: William Strahan, 1753.
Hymns of Intercession for All Mankind. London: J. Paramore, 1758.
Funeral Hymns. [Second Series.] London: Strahan, 1759.
Hymns for Those to Whom Christ is All in All. London, 1761.
Select Hymns with Tunes Annext. London, 1761.
———. [2nd ed.] London, 1765.
Short Hymns on Select Passages of the Holy Scriptures. 2 vols. Bristol: E. Farley, 1762.

An Epistle to the Reverend Mr George Whitefield: Written in the Year MDCCLV. London: J. and W. Oliver, 1771.

A Collection of Hymns for the Use of the People Called Methodists. London: J. Paramore, 1780.

———. 2nd ed. London: J. Paramore, 1781.

———. 5th ed. London: J. Paramore, 1786.

———. 7th ed. London, 1791.

Sacred Harmony or A Choice Collection of Psalm and Hymn Tunes. [London: 1780.]

A Pocket Hymn Book for the Use of Christians of All Denominations. London: J. Paramore, 1785.

———. [2nd ed.] London: J. Paramore, 1787.

OTHER RESOURCES

Adams, Nelson F. *The Musical Sources for John Wesley's Tunebooks: the Genealogy of 148 Tunes*. Dissertation, Union Theological Seminary, 1988.

Addison, Joseph. "When all Thy mercies, O my God." *The Spectator*, No. 453 (9 Aug. 1712) 317–319.

Allchin, A.M. "The Trinity in the Teaching of Charles Wesley: A Study in Eighteenth-Century Orthodoxy?" *Proceedings of The Charles Wesley Society* 4 (1997) 69–84.

Almond, Philip. "Western Images of Islam, 1700-1900." *Australian Journal of Politics and History* 49/3 (2003) 412–413.

Bailey, Albert Edward. *The Gospel in Hymns: Background and Interpretation*. New York: Charles Scribner's Sons, 1950.

Baker, Frank. *Charles Wesley as Revealed by His Letters*. London: Epworth, 1948.

———. *Representative Verse of Charles Wesley*. New York: Abingdon, 1962.

Baker, Frank, et al., eds. *The Works of John Wesley*. 32 vols. Nashville: Abingdon Press, 1984–2018.

Battishill, Jonathan. *Twelve Hymns, The Words by the Rev'd Mr. Charles Wesley M.A.* London: C. & S. Thompson, [1765].

Borgen, Ole E. *Wesley on the Sacraments: A Theological Study*. Nashville: Abingdon Press, 1972.

Boulainvilliers, Henri, Comte de. *The Life of Mahomet*. London: W. Hinchliffe, 1731.

Bowmer, John C. *The Sacrament of the Lord's Supper in Early Methodism*. London: Dacre, 1951.

Brailsford, Mabel R. *A Tale of Two Brothers: John & Charles Wesley*. New York: Oxford University Press, 1954.

Campbell, Ted A. *John Wesley and Christian Antiquity: Religious Vision and Cultural Change*. Nashville: Kingswood, 1991.

Charlesworth, James H. "The Wesleys and the Canon." *Proceedings of the Charles Wesley Society* 3 (1996) 63–88.

Chase, Frederic H. Jr. *Saint John of Damascus: Writings*. The Fathers of the Church 37. New York: Fathers of the Church, 1958.

Chilcote, Paul W. "'All the image of Thy love': Charles Wesley's vision of the one thing needful." *Proceedings of The Charles Wesley Society* 18 (2014) 21–40.

———. *A Faith That Sings: Biblical Themes in the Lyrical Theology of Charles Wesley*. Eugene, OR: Cascade, 2016.

———. "John and Charles Wesley." In *Christian Theologies of the Sacraments: A Comparative Introduction*, edited by Justin S. Holcomb and David A. Johnson, 272–94. New York: New York University Press, 2017.
Cotterell, F.P. "The Christology of Islam." In *Christ the Lord*, edited by Harold H. Rowdon, 290–295. Leicester: InterVarsity, 1982.
Curnock, Nehemiah. *The Journal of the Rev. John Wesley*. 8 vols. London: Epworth, 1938.
Darling, James. *Cyclopaedia Bibliographica*. London: James Darling, 1854.
Darsey, Steven. "John Wesley as Hymn and Tune Editor." *The Hymn* 47/1 (Jan. 1996) 17–24.
Daw, Carl P. Jr.. "Come, thou long-expected Jesus." In *Glory to God: A Companion*, 82–84. Louisville: Westminster John Knox, 2016.
Dudley-Smith, Timothy. "Come, O thou traveller unknown." In *The Canterbury Dictionary of Hymnology*, edited by J.R. Watson and Emma Hornby. London: Canterbury, n.d. http://www.hymnology.co.uk/c/come,-o-thou-traveller-unknown.
Duncan, J. Ligon. "Come, Thou Long Expected Jesus." In *First Presbyterian Church* (Jackson, MS). https://www.fpcjackson.org/resource-library/sermons/come-thou-long-expected-jesus.
Eddy, G.T. *Dr. Taylor of Norwich: Wesley's Arch-heretic*. Peterborough: Epworth, 2003.
Fenner, Chris. "Joy to the world." In *Hymnology Archive* (13 Dec. 2018). https://www.hymnologyarchive.com/joy-to-the-world.
———. "Surrexit Christus Hodie." In *Hymnology Archive* (22 June 2018). https://www.hymnologyarchive.com/surrexit-christus-hodie.
Haleem, M.A.S. Abdel. *The Qur'ān*. Oxford: University Press, 2004.
Hawn, C. Michael. "Come, O thou traveller unknown." In *History of Hymns*. Discipleship Ministries, The United Methodist Church. https://www.umcdiscipleship.org/resources/history-of-hymns-come-o-thou-traveler-unknown.
———. "Hymn expresses longing for arrival of our Savior." In *History of Hymns*. Discipleship Ministries, The United Methodist Church. https://www.umcdiscipleship.org/resources/history-of-hymns-hymn-expresses-longing-for-arrival-of-our-savior.
Hicks, Anthony. "George Frederic Handel." In *Grove Music Online* (20 Jan. 2001). https://doi.org/10.1093/gmo/9781561592630.article.40060.
Holman, Peter. "John Frederick Lampe." In *Grove Music Online* (20 Jan. 2001). Oxford University Press. https://doi.org/10.1093/gmo/9781561592630.article.O007823.
The Homes, Haunts, and Friends of John Wesley. Revised and Enlarged. London: Charles H. Kelly, 1891.
Hunt, Mark E., and Hughes M. Huffman. *Carols*. Downers Grove, IL: InterVarsity, 1978.
Hymns and Psalms. London: Methodist Publishing House, 1983.
Hymns on the Great Festivals. Madison, NJ: Charles Wesley Society, 1996.
Jackson, Thomas, ed. *The Works of the Rev. John Wesley, A.M.* 3rd ed. 14 vols. London: John Mason, 1829–1831.
———. *The Journal of the Rev. Charles Wesley, M.A.* London: John Mason, 1849.
Jacobs, Horace Lincoln. "A rescue of two centuries ago." *The Epworth Herald* 19/37 (6 February 1909) 15.
John Julian, ed. *A Dictionary of Hymnology*. London: J. Murray, 1892.
Kimbrough, S.T. *A Heart to Praise My God: Wesley Hymns for Today*. Nashville: Abingdon, 1996.

———. *The Lyrical Theology of Charles Wesley*. Expanded Ed. Eugene, OR: Cascade, 2013.

Kimbrough, S.T., and Oliver A. Beckerlegge, eds. *The Unpublished Poetry of Charles Wesley*. 3 vols. Nashville: Kingswood, 1988–1992.

Kimbrough, S.T., and Kenneth G.C. Newport, eds. *The Manuscript Journal of the Reverend Charles Wesley, M.A.* Nashville: Kingswood Books, 2008.

Knight, Henry H. III. "Wesley and the Doctrinal Role of Hymnody." In *Catalyst: Contemporary Evangelical Perspectives for United Methodists Seminarians* (1 February 2005). https://www.catalystresources.org/consider-wesley-27/.

Langford, Thomas A. "Charles Wesley as Theologian." In *Charles Wesley: Poet and Theologian*, edited by S. T. Kimbrough, Jr., 97–105. Nashville: Abingdon Press, 1992.

Larrabee, William Clark. *Wesley and His Coadjutors*. Cincinnati: Swormstedt & Poe, 1853.

Law, William. *A Practical Treatise Upon Christian Perfection*. London: William and John Innys, 1726.

———. *A Serious Call to a Devout and Holy Life*. London: William Innys, 1729.

Lawson, John. *A Thousand Tongues: The Wesley Hymns as a Guide to Scriptural Teaching*. London: Paternoster, 1987.

Lightwood, James T. *Methodist Music in the Eighteenth Century*. London: Epworth, 1927.

Louth, Andrew. *St. John Damascene: Tradition and Originality in Byzantine Theology*. Oxford: University Press, 2002.

Luther, Martin. *Dr. Martin Luther's Commentary Upon the Epistle to the Galatians*. London: J. Brotherton, 1734.

Madan, Martin. *A Collection of Psalms and Hymns Extracted from Various Authors*. London: 1760.

Maddox, Randy L., ed. *Charles Wesley's Manuscript Verse*. Durham, NC: Duke Divinity School. https://divinity.duke.edu/initiatives/cswt/charles-manuscript-verse.

———. *Charles Wesley's Published Verse*. Durham, NC: Duke Divinity School. https://divinity.duke.edu/initiatives/cswt/charles-published-verse.

———. *John Wesley's Poetry, Hymn, and Verse*. Durham, NC: Duke Divinity School. https://divinity.duke.edu/initiatives/cswt/john-wesley.

Martin, Dennis R. *The Operas and Operatic Style of John Frederick Lampe*. Detroit: Monographs in Musicology, 1985.

Mason, John, ed. *A Collection of Hymns for the Use of the People Called Methodists*, with Supplement. London: John Mason, 1831.

Meistad, Tore. "The Missiology of Charles Wesley: An Introduction." *Proceedings of The Charles Wesley Society* 5 (1998) 37–59.

———. "The Missiology of Charles Wesley and Its Links to the Eastern Church." In *Orthodox and Wesleyan Spirituality*, edited by S.T. Kimbrough, 205–31. Crestwood, NY: St. Vladimir's Seminary, 2002.

The Methodist Hymnal. Cincinnati: Methodist Pulishing House, 1932.

Mitchell, T. Crichton. *Charles Wesley: Man with the Dancing Heart*. Kansas City: Beacon Hill Press, 1994.

Najapfour, Brian G. "'Where Shall My Wondering Soul Begin?': A Historical and Theological Analysis." *Puritan Reformed Journal* 3.2 (2011) 291–98.

Newport, Kenneth G.C., and Gareth Lloyd, eds. *The Letters of Charles Wesley: Volume I, 1728-1756.* Oxford: University Press, 2013.

Newton, John A. "Brothers in Arms: The Partnership of John and Charles Wesley." In *Charles Wesley: Life, Literature, & Legacy,* edited by Kenneth G.C. Newport and Ted Campbell, 58-69. Werrington: Epworth, 2007.

Nichols, Stephen J. *Pages from Church History.* New Jersey: P&R Publishing, 2006.

Parkinson, John A. "Michael Arne." In *Grove Music Online* (20 Jan. 2001). Oxford University Press. https://doi.org/10.1093/gmo/9781561592630.article.01286.

Parrinder, Geoffrey. *Jesus in the Qur'ān.* New York: Barnes & Noble, 1965.

Prideaux, Humphrey. *The True Nature of Imposture Fully Display'd in the Life of Mahomet.* 2nd ed. London: William Rogers, 1697.

Rattenbury, J. Ernest. *The Conversions of the Wesleys: A Critical Study.* London: Epworth, 1938.

———. *The Eucharistic Hymns of John and Charles Wesley.* London: Epworth, 1948.

———. *The Evangelical Doctrines of Charles Wesley's Hymns.* London: Epworth, 1941.

Richie, Tony. "John Wesley and Mohammed: A Contemporary Inquiry Concerning Islam." *The Asbury Theological Journal* 58/2 (Fall 2003) 79-99.

Sahas, Daniel J. *John of Damascus on Islam: The "Heresy of the Ishmaelites."* Leiden: E.J. Brill, 1972.

Sanchez, Diana, ed. *The Hymns of the Methodist Hymnal.* Nashville: Abingdon Press, 1989.

Schmidt, Martin. *John Wesley: A Theological Biography.* Translated by Denis Inman. Nashville: Abingdon, 1966.

Severance, Diane. "Charles Wesley." In *Christianity.com* (28 April 2010). https://www.christianity.com/church/church-history/timeline/1701-1800/charles-wesley-11630230.html.

Spurgeon, Charles H. "The Incarnation and birth of Christ." In *New Park Street Pulpit* 2, 25-32. London: Passmore & Alabaster, 1856.

———. *Our Own Hymn-Book.* London: Passmore & Alabaster, 1866.

———. *The Two Wesleys.* Pasadena: Pilgrim Publications, 1975.

Stevenson, Robert. "The Eighteenth-Century Hymn Tune." *Inter-American Music Review* 2/1 (Fall 1979) 1-33.

Stevick, David B. *The Altar's Fire: Charles Wesley's Hymns on the Lord's Supper, 1745, Introduction and Exposition.* Peterborough: Epworth, 2004.

Taylor, Justin. "George Whitefield's Gospel-Centered Hymn Book." In *The Gospel Coalition* (13 June 2017). https://www.thegospelcoalition.org/blogs/evangelical-history/george-whitefields-hymn-book/.

Telford, John, ed. *The Letters of the Rev. John Wesley, A.M.* 8 vols. London: Epworth, 1960.

Temperley, Nicholas, ed. *The Hymn Tune Index.* http://hymntune.library.uiuc.edu.

Toplady, Augustus. *Psalms and Hymns for Public and Private Worship.* London: E. & C. Dilly, 1776.

Tyson, John R. *Assist Me to Proclaim: The Life and Hymns of Charles Wesley.* Grand Rapids: Eerdmans, 2007.

———. *Charles Wesley: A Reader.* Oxford: University Press, 1989.

———. *Charles Wesley on Sanctification: A Biographical and Theological Study.* Grand Rapids: Francis Asbury, 1987.

———. "'I Preached the Cross as Usual': Charles Wesley and Redemption." In *Charles Wesley: Life, Literature, & Legacy*, edited by Kenneth G.C. Newport and Ted Campbell, 204-28. Werrington: Epworth, 2007.

The United Methodist Hymnal. Nashville: United Methodist Publishing House, 1989.

Watson, J.R. *An Annotated Anthology of Hymns.* Oxford: University Press, 2002.

———. *The English Hymn: A Critical and Historical Study.* Oxford: Clarendon Press, 1997.

———. "Welkins." In *Bulletin*, Hymn Society of Great Britain and Ireland 16/3 (July 2000) 80.

Welsey, John. *Christian Perfection: A Sermon.* London: Strahan, 1741.

———. "The Means of Grace." In *Sermons on Several Occasions*, 1:225–250. London: William Strahan, 1746.

———. *Sunday Service of the Methodists in North America.* London: William Strahan, 1784.

Wesley, Samuel. *The Fitzwilliam Music, Never Published, Three Hymns, the Words by the late Revd Charles Wesley, A.M . . . Set to Music by George Frederick Handel.* London: S. Wesley, 1826.

Whitefield, George. *A Collection of Hymns for Social Worship.* London: William Strahan, 1753.

———. *A Collection of Hymns for Social Worship.* 5th ed. London: William Strahan, 1756.

Wilson, John. "Handel and the Hymn Tune: I. Handel's Tunes for Charles Wesley's Hymns." *The Hymn* 36/4 (Oct. 1985) 18–23.

———. "Handel and the Hymn Tune: II. Some Hymn Tune Arrangements." *The Hymn* 37/1 (Jan. 1986): 25–31.

———. "Handel's Tunes for Charles Wesley's hymns: the Story Retold." *Bulletin*, The Hymn Society of Great Britain & Ireland 11/2 (May 1985) 32–37.

Young, Carlton R. *Companion to The United Methodist Hymnal.* Nashville: Abingdon Press, 1993.

———. *Music of the Heart: John & Charles Wesley on Music and Musicians.* Carol Stream, IL: Hope, 1995.

Subject Index

Absolution, 36
Adam, 14, 60, 62–63, 68, 108, 148, 158–59, 161
Addison, Joseph, 92
Akeroyde, Samuel, 141, 147
America. *See* Georgia mission.
Antinomianism, 74, 78
Arminianism, 10
Arne, Thomas Augustine, 111, 114, 117, 119, 123, 129, 143, 169
Arnold, Samuel, 126
Assurance, 15, 21–23, 34–35, 89
Atonement, 10, 13, 15, 16, 20, 22, 48, 56, 149

Babcock, Maltbie, 131
Bach, Johann Christian, 113n7
Battishill, C. Jonathan, 117, 129
Blackwell, Ebenezer, 120
Böhler, Peter, 23n13, 39
Book of Common Prayer, 80n4, 92, 100
Borgen, Ole, 83
Boulainvilliers, Henri Comte de, 98
Boyce, William, 114
Bray, John, 6, 19–20
Brevint, Daniel, 81
Bunyan, John, 135
Butts, Thomas, 114, 119–20, 127, 141–42

Callcott, J.W., 126
Calvinism, 10, 49, 51
Carey, Henry, 118, 129, 144

Cennick, John, 21
Church, Thomas, 77n10
Claggett, Metcalf, 21
Clayton, John, 73
Communion, 3, 20, 73, 78, 79–85, 163
Confirmation, 80
Conversion, 80
    of Charles, 3–10, 11–17, 18–26, 33, 39, 64

Darsey, Steven, 112
Davies, Cecelia, 113
Daw, Carl Jr., 52
Dryden, John, 87, 114–15, 143
Dudley-Smith, Timothy, 40
Duncan, J. Ligon, 54

Edwards, Jonathan, 106
Evangelism, 14, 19, 23

Fitzwilliam Museum, 124

Georgia mission, 3, 19, 31–32, 39, 53, 59, 74
Gerhardt, Paul, 126
Giardini, Felice de, 113n7
Grace, 4, 5, 7, 11, 13–14, 16, 18, 21, 23–24, 33–34, 42, 83, 108, 150, 152, 162, 164–65, 170–71
    Free grace, 11, 19, 148
    Grace alone, 33, 74, 78
    Inward grace, 80
    Unfathomable, 82
Great Commission, 55n29

Handel, George Frideric, 111–12, 114, 117–19, 123–29, 160, 173
Hawn, C. Michael, 52
Henry, Matthew, 38
High Priest, 16
Hille, Johann Georg, 143, 163
Holcombe, Henry, 141, 154
Holford, William, 128
Holland, William, 11, 20
Holy Club, 3, 59, 73
Hunt, Mark E., 57
Hypostasis, 13

Incarnation, 14, 47–58, 59–63, 88, 93
Ingham, Benjamin, 73
Islam, 97–108, 168

Jacob, 36–43
John of Damascus, 107
Joshua (high priest), 16
Journal entries, Charles
   2 August 1736, 53
   28 October 1736, 31–32
   11 May 1738, 19
   16 May 1738, 20
   17 May 1738, 11, 20
   19 May 1738, 20
   20 May 1738, 20
   21 May 1738, 3, 20–21, 23, 33
   22 May 1738, 4, 23
   23 May 1738, 3, 6, 7
   26 September 1740, 89
Journal entries, John
   29 November 1745, 119
   5 November 1755, 50
   23 November 1767, 99
   18 November 1770, 50
   2 January 1771, 50
Justification, 10–12, 16, 20, 24, 33, 74, 84, 150

Kelway, Joseph, 113
Kenosis, 14
Kerygma, 19, 24
Kimbrough, S.T., 53, 83, 84
Knibb, Thomas, 117, 143
Knight, Henry H. III, 92
Krieger, Adam, 142, 162

Lampe, John Frederick, 87, 111, 114, 117–24, 129, 139–40, 143–44, 166, 171
Law, William, 73, 89
Letters to/from Charles
   28 February 1738 (Samuel W.), 19n6
   11 December 1746 (E. Blackwell), 120
   8 October 1749 (E. Blackwell), 49–50
   Whitsunday 1760 (Sarah W.), 21
   9 July 1764 (John W.), 89–90
   28 April 1785 (Dr. Chandler), 80
Letters to/from John
   9 December 1758 (A. Toplady), 102, 107
   9 July 1764 (Charles W.), 89–90
Lord's Supper. *See* Communion.
Luther, Martin, 11–12, 20, 74

Macleod, Norman, 131
Madan, Martin, 49, 61, 63, 93, 151
Maddox, Randy L., 49, 64, 86, 90
Mary, mother of Christ, 63
Mary Magdalene, 8
Mason, Lowell, 128
Means of Grace, 73–78, 79–84, 142, 162
Mitchell, T. Crichton, 47, 48–49
Molther, Philip, 74
Montgomery, James, 127
Moravians, 3, 23n13, 39, 74
Muhammad, 97–108, 168

Neumark, Georg, 143, 146, 168
Nichols, Stephen J., 47

Oxford University, 3, 59, 73, 80
Owen, John, 135

Patripassianism, 9, 13
Paul (the apostle), 12–13, 35, 69–70
Pentecost, 13, 19–22, 33, 39
Perfection, 18, 84, 89–90, 93
Peter (the apostle), 13, 33
Pilate, Pontius 66–67
Predestination, 49

SUBJECT INDEX 185

Prideaux, Humphrey, 97–102
Propitiation, 16
Purcell, Henry, 87, 114–16, 129, 143, 165

Rattenbury, J. Ernest, 5, 39, 48, 83
Redemption, 4, 5, 10, 19, 23–24, 52, 54, 57–58, 66, 92, 103, 146, 150, 159, 161
Resurrection, 34–35, 54, 56, 63, 64–70, 159–61
Rich, John & Priscilla, 118, 123, 129
Rider, Charles, 128

Sacraments, 20, 73–78, 79–85, 162–63
Salvation, 5–8, 11, 13, 18–26, 48, 55, 57, 74, 86–87, 103, 147, 150, 164–66
  by grace, 24, 74, 77, 78, 150
Sanctification, 19, 68, 84, 86, 89, 91, 152, 164–65
Satan, 6–7, 101–2, 147, 167–68
Simpson, John, 74
Slavery, 53
Somerville, William, 60
Spiritual disciplines, 73, 78, 81
Spurgeon, Charles H., 50–51
Stillness doctrine, 74
Storms, 29–35, 151

Taylor, John, 106–7
Temperley, Nicholas, 126
Tersteegen, Gerhardt, 143
Tiplady, Thomas, 131
Tolkien, J.R.R., 60
Toplady, Augustus, 49, 93, 107
Truett, George W., 131
Tyson, John R., 20, 21, 86, 103, 105

United Brethren. *See* Moravians.

Watson, J.R., 37, 39, 61, 87, 93

Watts, Isaac, 36–37, 39, 67n11, 127–28, 132, 141
Wesley, John
  Against Calvinism, 49
  Against Unitarianism, 106–7
  at death of Charles, 39–40
  Editor and compiler, 63, 92–93, 126, 139
  Epworth fire, 5
  Georgia mission, 3, 39
  Journal entries, 50, 99, 119
  Letters, 89–90, 102, 107
  Literary output, 132, 136
  Means of grace, 74
  Musical taste, 111–12
  Oxford Holy Club, 73
  Perfection controversy, 89–90, 93
  Preaching and sermons, 47
  Sacraments, 80
  Shadow over Charles, ix, 47, 132, 136
  Spiritual renewal, 79
  Translator, 126, 143
  and Thomas Church, 77n10
  and Paul Gerhardt, 126
  and J.F. Lampe, 119–20
  and Martin Madan, 61
  and Muhammad (Islam), 98–108
  and Charles Spurgeon, 51
  and John Taylor, 106–7
  and George Whitefield, 49–50
Wesley, Samuel (son), 124
Wesley, Samuel Jr. (brother), 8, 19n6
Wesley, Sarah (wife), 21–22
Wesley, Sarah (daughter), 123–24
Whitefield, George, 10, 21, 38, 49–50, 59, 61–63, 73, 88n7, 141
Whitsunday. *See* Pentecost.
Williams, Aaron, 128
Wilson, John, 125

Young, Carlton R., 39, 112

Collections and Hymns Index

COLLECTIONS

100 Hymns for Today (1969), 125

African Methodist Episcopal Hymn and Tune Book (1898), 128
Anglican Hymnbook (1868) 125

The BBC Hymn Book (1951), 125
British Psalmody, Aaron Williams (1785), 128

Carols, M. Hunt (1978), 57
A Collection of Hymns (1742), 11
A Collection of Hymns and Sacred Poems, J.F. Lampe (1749), 120, 140, 142, 149
A Collection of Hymns for Social Worship, G. Whitefield (1753), 50, 61, 88n7
A Collection of Hymns for the Use of the People Called Methodists (1780), 4, 11, 21, 37, 61, 74, 92, 99, 105, 115, 117–18, 122, 126, 128, 140–43, 148, 150, 154, 165, 166, 168, 171, 173–74
———, 2nd ed. (1781), 4, 146, 162
———, 5th ed. (1786), 140
A Collection of Psalm and Hymn Tunes, M. Madan (1760–63), 141
A Collection of Psalms and Hymns (1737), 92
A Collection of Psalms and Hymns, M. Madan (1760), 49, 61, 65n6, 93

A Collection of Tunes . . . Sung at the Foundery (1742), 11, 64–65, 112, 119, 126, 139–44, 147, 159

Divine Musical Miscellany (1754), 88, 123, 141

The English Hymnal (1906), 125
An Epistle to the Reverend Mr George Whitefield (1771), 50

Foundery Collection. See *A Collection of Tunes* (1742).
Funeral Hymns, Second Series (1759), 120–22

Gloria Patri; or Hymns to the Trinity (1746), 48, 105–6
Graces Before and After Meat (1747), 120, 140

Harmonia Sacra, T. Butts (1753, etc.), 114, 119–20, 123, 127, 141–42
Hymnal 1982 (1985), 127
Hymns Ancient & Modern, rev. (1950)
Hymns and Psalms (1983), 65n6, 125
Hymns and Sacred Poems (1739), 4, 11, 59, 64, 140, 142–43
———, 2nd ed. (1739), 61
———, 4th ed. (1743), 4, 64, 159–60
Hymns and Sacred Poems (1740), 21, 30, 74, 100–101

Hymns and Sacred Poems (1742), 37, 128, 141, 143–44
Hymns and Sacred Poems (1747), 11, 64
Hymns and Sacred Poems (1749), 18, 117, 141–42
Hymns and Spiritual Songs, I. Watts (1707), 141
Hymns and Spiritual Songs (1753), 4, 21, 30, 37, 74
Hymns for Our Lord's Resurrection (1746), 143
Hymns for the Nativity of Our Lord (1745), 48, 141, 156
Hymns for Those that Seek (1747), 86, 100, 120, 140
Hymns for Those to Whom Christ is All in All (1761), 4, 11, 90
Hymns Occasioned by the Earthquake, Pt. 1 (1750), 144
Hymns of Intercession for All Mankind (1758), 99, 108, 118, 144
Hymns on the Great Festivals (1746), 18, 86–87, 114, 119–20, 122, 124, 129, 139, 143–44, 166
Hymns on the Lord's Supper (1745), 79, 81, 143, 163

Introduction to Psalmody, J. Church (1723), 118

Lyra Davidica (1708), 65n4, 142, 157, 159

Methodist Hymnal (1876, 1889), 125
Methodist Hymnal (1932), 130–37
Methodist Hymn Book (1933), 125, 127

Nativity Hymns. See *Hymns for the Nativity* (1745).

Occasional Psalm and Hymn Tunes (1836), 128
Our Own Hymn-Book, C.H. Spurgeon (1866), 51

A Pocket Hymn Book (1785), 30, 61, 140, 151

———, rev. ed. (1787), 21, 61, 118, 140, 142, 157
Presbyterian Hymnal (1990), 127
Psalm Singer's Help, T. Knibb (1769), 117, 143
Psalmodia Britannica, C. Rider (1831), 128
Psalms and Hymns for Public and Private Worship, A. Toplady (1776), 49, 93
The Psalms of David for the Use of Parish Churches (1791), 126

Sacred Harmony (1780), 64, 112, 117–20, 123, 127, 140–44, 146, 148, 151, 154, 157, 160, 162–63, 165, 168, 169, 171, 173–74
School Hymn Book (1950), 125
Select Hymns with Tunes Annext (1761), 30, 87–88, 90, 111–12, 114, 118–19, 122–23, 139–44
———, rev. ed. (1765), 117, 139–43, 156
A Selection of Psalm and Hymn Tunes, J. Rippon (1792), 128, 142
Short Hymns on Select Passages of the Holy Scriptures (1762), 104, 143–44, 169
Songs of Praise (1931), 125
Supplement to the New Version, Tate & Brady (1700)

Trinity Psalter Hymnal (2018), 127
Twelve Hymns, J. Battishill (1765), 117

United Methodist Hymnal (1989), 36–37, 39, 65n6, 118, 125

Voce di Melodia, W. Holford (1833), 128

HYMNS
"Above the hills of time," 131
"Ah! lovely appearance of death," 123
"All glory to God in the sky," 117
"All praise to thee, my God, this night," 131
"And are we yet alive," 19, 136

"And can it be that I should gain," 9, 11–17, 118, 122, 141, 147–49
"And let our bodies part," 136
"Awake, our souls; away, our fears," 127

"Be strong, we are not here to play," 131
"Blest be the dear uniting love," 137
"But above all, lay hold," 126

"Christ, from whom all blessings flow," 122
"Christ the Lord is ris'n today," 64–70, 93, 118, 132, 136, 142, 159–161
"Christ, whose glory fills the skies," 100n14, 136
"Come, holy, celestial Dove," 117
"Come, Holy Ghost, our hearts inspire," 137
"Come, let us anew our journey pursue," 136
"Come, let us sing the song of songs," 127
"Come, O thou traveller unknown," 36–43, 136, 141, 152–55
"Come, thou long-expected Jesus," 47–58, 136, 141, 156
"Come on, my partners in distress" (sts. 5–6), 106n37, 141
"Come on, my Whitefield!" 50
"Come, sinners, to the gospel feast," 136
"Commit thou all thy griefs," 126
"Courage brother! Do not stumble," 131

"Enslav'd to sense, to pleasure prone," 142

"Father of all, above, below" (st. 2), 105
"Father of Jesus Christ, my Lord," 127
"Father of light, from whom proceeds," 140–41
"Forth in thy name, O Lord, I go," 133, 137
"From whence these dire portents around," 144

"Glory be to God on high," 142
"Glory to God the Father give," 105n34
"Glory to Him who freely spent" (st. 4), 80
"God of all power, and truth, and grace" (st. 28), 89
"God of unexampled grace," 143
"Gott ist gegenwärtig," 143

"Hail, Father, Son, and Spirit great" (st. 2), 105n36
"Hail the day that sees him rise," 122
"Happy soul, that free from harms," 117
"Hark, a voice divides the sky," 122
"Hark! the herald angels sing," 49, 59–63, 65, 94, 132, 136, 142, 157–58
"He comes! he comes! the Judge severe," 118, 144, 170
"Head of the church triumphant," 122
"Holy, holy, holy Lord" (st. 3), 105n34
"How sad our state by nature is!" 142

"I know that my Redeemer lives," 128
"I long to behold him arrayed," 117
"I want a principle within," 131, 136, 144, 174–75
"I will hearken what my Lord," 143
"In fellowship alone," 126
"Infinite God, to thee we raise," 123

"Jesu, help thy fallen creature," 142
"Jesu, let thy pitying eye," 122
"Jesu, lover of my soul," 29–35, 93, 132, 137, 141, 151–52
"Jesu, show us thy salvation," 87, 143
"Jesu, thy boundless love to me," 118
"Jesus Christ is risen today," 65
"Jesus, Lord, we look to thee," 127
"Jesus, my strength and righteousness," 100n14
"Jesus, my strength, my hope," 136
"Jesus, thine all victorious love," 136
"Jesus, thou art the mighty God" (st. 2), 105
"Jesus, thou soul of all our joys," 125
"Jesus, we look to thee," 136

"Joy to the world, the Lord is come," 128
"Lamb of God, whose bleeding love," 122
"Let the world their virtue boast," 122
"Lo, God is here; let us adore," 143
"Lord God, your love has called us here," 118
"Lord over all, if thou hast made," 108
"Lord, regard my earnest cry," 122
"Love divine, all loves excelling," 86–94, 114, 118, 136, 143–44, 164–66
"Loving Saviour, Prince of peace," 115
"The Means of Grace," 73–78, 142, 162

"Meet and right it is to praise," 122
"My Father, O my Father, hear," 143

"Nun sich der Tag geendet hat," 142

"O for a heart to praise my God," 136
"O for a thousand tongues to sing," 18–26, 93, 100–101, 135–36, 141, 150
"O how happy are they who the Savior obey," 135–36
"O love divine, how sweet thou art," 123, 125
"O love divine, what hast thou done?" 141
"O the depth of love divine," 79–85, 143, 162–63
"Oh, that thou would'st the heavens rend," 144
"On the Death of a Believer," 123

"Rejoice for a brother deceased," 127
"Rejoice, the Lord is King," 93, 123, 125

"Savior, breathe an evening blessing," 131
"Sei willkommen, sei willkommen, Jesulein, mein freund," 143
"Sing to the great Jehovah's praise," 136

"Sinners, obey the gospel word," 18, 118, 122, 125, 144, 171
"Sinners, turn, why will ye die?"
"Spirit of Faith, come down,"
"Soldiers of Christ, arise," 126, 128, 144, 172–73
"Sun of unclouded righteousness," 97–108, 143, 167–68
"Superior to all fear and shame" (st. 3), 104
"Surrexit Christus hodie," 65

"The Lord my pasture shall prepare," 118
"Thee, Father of men" (st. 4), 106
"Thee, Father, Son, and Holy Ghost," 105
"Thee we adore, eternal name," 141
"Thou hidden source of calm repose," 122, 141
"Thou Shepherd of Israel, and mine," 117, 143, 168–69
"'Tis done! the Sovereign will's obey'd," 120–22
"'Tis finished, 'tis done," 123
"Trust in God, and do the right!" 131

"Wer nur den lieben Gott läßt walten," 143
"What are these arrayed in white," 117
"What now is my object and aim?" 117
"When all thy mercies, O my God," 92
"When I survey the wondrous cross," 67n11, 128
"When morning guilds the skies," 131
"Where shall my wondering soul begin?" 3–10, 39, 140–41, 146–47
"While shepherds watched their flocks by night," 126
"Why did my dying Lord ordain" (st. 4), 81
"The Woman of Canaan," 122

"Ye servants of God, your master proclaim," 123

Scripture Index

Genesis
1:2	32
3:7	16
3:15	63
32:24–32	37–39

Exodus
10:21–22	101
23:21	38
33:22	32

Ruth
2:12	32

1 Samuel
15:29	55

Job
38:8–11	32

Psalms
2:6	68
2:12	68
5:11	32
9:9–10	32
17:8	32
29:11	54
46:1–3	32, 55, 76
68:35	55
91:4	32
106:4	88
139:23	56

Isaiah
1:1–20	78
7:14	54, 63, 88
9:6–7	54, 63
40:1	20
43:1–3	4, 32
53	54
61:1	54
64:6–7	56

Ezekiel
36:27	56

Hosea
12:4	38
13:14	67n10

Micah
5:2	54

Haggai
2:7	53, 63

Zechariah
3:1–5	16
3:2	5

Malachi

3:7	74
4:2	63, 100

Matthew

1:21	55
1:23	88
5:48	89
6:10	56
8:23–27	32
9:13	8
11:28	9
11:29	54
14:30–31	33
22:37–39	84
24:12	74
27:66	66

Mark

4:39	32
13:26	56
15:34	104
16:6	65

Luke

1:33	56
2:8–21	62
2:10	57
4:18	54
7:36–50	8
8:12	8
19:10	8
23:43	67
23:45	66

John

1:14	63, 88
3	63
5:24	55
10:10	93
14:6	55
14:23	88
20:22	89

Acts

1:8	55n29
2:23	13
2:42–44	74
20:28	13

Romans

1:16	104n28
3:23	56
3:25	16
5:20	34
6:4–8	35
6:9–11	66
6:23	56
8:1	16
8:2	54

1 Corinthians

2:8	67
6:19	91
15	63
15:20	67
15:22	68
15:45–49	63
15:55	67

2 Corinthians

3:18	92
4:6	88
5:21	16
12:9	55

Galatians

2:20	12, 20, 34, 63

Ephesians

1:22	67
2:1–4	15
3:17–19	88
5:27	93

Philippians

2:5–8	63, 88
3:10	69

Colossians

3:1–2	68
3:3–4	69

1 Timothy

1:14	34
1:15	54
6:15	56

2 Timothy

4:8	88

Hebrews

12:2	89
13:8	62

James

1:12	88
2:17	78

1 Peter

1:12	13
2:9–10	55
3:19–20	66
5:4	88

1 John

2:2	16
3:1	6
4:10	16
5:10	15

Revelation

1:5	56
1:6	56
2:10	88
7:14	25
17:14	56
19:16	56
21:3	91
21:6	35
22:13	89
22:20	54, 91

www.ingramcontent.com/pod-product-compliance
Lightning Source LLC
Chambersburg PA
CBHW062038220426
43662CB00010B/1545